I. An entrance to Kensington Place and Gardens during the Regency; attributed to Her Royal Highness Princess Sophia.

LONDON GREEN

The story of Kensington Gardens, Hyde Park,
Green Park & St. James's Park

by

NEVILLE BRAYBROOKE

LONDON
VICTOR GOLLANCZ LTD
1959

B59   14859

To

JUNE

Printed in Great Britain by
The Camelot Press Ltd., London and Southampton

I have made a heap of all [the things] that I could find . . . lest they should be dissipated like smoke. . . . Partly from the writings and monuments of the ancient inhabitants of Britain, partly from the annals of the Romans and the chronicles of the sacred fathers . . . and [partly] from the histories of . . . the Saxons. . . . I have lispingly put together this . . . about past transactions, so that [such matters] might not be trodden under foot.

From the *Works* of GILDAS and NENNIUS (*fl.* 796).

There is a twofold meaning in every creature, a literal and a mystical, and the one is but the ground of the other; and as the Jews say of their law, so a good man says of everything that his senses offer him—it speaks to his lower part, but it points out something above to his mind and spirit. . . . A good man finds every place he treads upon holy ground. . . .

From *The Excellency and Nobleness of True Religion*, by JOHN SMITH (*c.* 1661).

Art is Nature. Art is Movement. Art is Colour. Everything is new the whole time.

From an interview with PAU CASALS on his 80th birthday (28th December, 1956).

PREFACE

LONDON GREEN stretches from the south-eastern tip of St. James's Park, at Storey's Gate, to the far north-western corner of Kensington Gardens, at Bull's Gate. Such at least is the geographical explanation of my title. Yet apart from telling the story of these four royal parks (later I hope to turn to those of Regent's, Greenwich, Richmond and Bushy), I have also tried to interpret their lie in the land; to show why each, with its particular character, has attracted a particular kind of person and hence history.

'If I doe anything you shall find mee to acknowledge and thank him that lighted mee a candle.' What an admirable precept that is from John Donne, and so first I must record my great debt to Jacob Larwood who set out to tell *The Story of the London Parks* nearly eighty years ago; even though his account stops short in the year 1825 and even though some of his conclusions are debatable, his early researches still remain invaluable. Other writers to whom I am no less indebted are listed in the 'Select Bibliography' at the end. Nor must I forget the many who perforce must be anonymous—the park rangers themselves, or the Metropolitan Police who have a station in the centre of Hyde Park. Much of what they told me is hearsay, the information that is passed from one generation to another and is seldom chronicled. For in writing this kind of book, who can say how much is discovered by chance—by overhearing the conversations of the old ladies who gather in Kensington's Flower Walk, or by recalling the anecdotes learnt at a grandmother's knee? In particular, before the war, I remember a long talk with a taxi-driver who had once been one of the cabbies on a rank north of Green Park.

For lending me many rare books about London and books of illustrations I am most grateful to my cousin Mr. Angus Bellairs, to Fr. Anselm Cooney of the Carmelite Order, and to Miss Barbara Jones. Here too I must include the staff of the British Museum Reading

Room who tracked down several items, and the Bailiff of the Royal Parks who answered many questions of an administrative order. The Ministry of Works (through their Officer of Information) kindly supplied me with detailed reports of any changes that occurred, such as the reasons for building a new bridge over the lake of St. James's.

I must thank the Editor of the *Manchester Guardian* for permission to reprint certain sections of Chapter II which originally appeared in his paper; I must also thank Mr. J. R. Ackerley and his publishers, the House of Secker & Warburg, for permission to quote from *My Dog Tulip: Life with an Alsatian* in Chapter IV.

In choosing the illustrations and maps I am most indebted to Miss Livia Gollancz for much patience and advice. Among the water-colours, prints and cartoons reproduced, Plates XV, XVIII, XIX, XXV, XXXIV, XLIII-XLV and XLIX are from the Crace Collection by the generous permission of the Trustees of the British Museum; Plates XXVI-XXVIII by the generous permission of the Trustees of the Victoria & Albert Museum; Plates XX, XXIB, XXXII, XXXIII, XXXV, XXXVI, XXXVIII, XLII, XLVI and XLVIII by the generous permission of the Westminster Library local history department; and Plates I-VI, VII-XII, XVI, XVII, XXII-XXIV, XXX and XXXI by the generous permission of the Kensington Public Library, VI and XVI being copies of water-colours in the possession of Mr. Geoffrey Agnew. To Mr. C. G. Boxall, the Reference Librarian at Kensington, I should like to add an extra word of gratitude for the time that he so willingly put at my disposal.

For typing my MS. with such efficiency I must thank Mrs. Grace Ginnis; and for preparing the end-paper maps with such care I must thank Miss Joan Emerson.

Lastly, to my wife I owe a very special debt of gratitude. Had it not been for her constant encouragement and love, I should have given up this project long ago: 'More is thy due than more than all can pay.'

N. B.

HAMPSTEAD.
January, 1959

Postscript. Throughout this book, save in quotations where I follow the precedents set by the authors in question, I write St. James's Park with an apostrophe followed by an *s*. My rule is based on sound. Thus it is that on one page I refer to 'Samuel Rogers' house', on another to 'the Duchess's major-domo'.

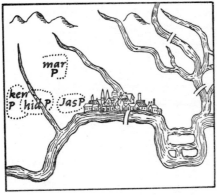

A map of London, reproduced from a Civil War Tract, showing the size of the parks in relation to the rest of the city in 1642.

CONTENTS

LIST OF ILLUSTRATIONS

The end-papers provide a map of the parks today; four other maps, listed below, show the state of the parks in the seventeenth and eighteenth centuries; a map of London, reproduced on page 9 from a Civil War Tract, shows the size of the parks in relation to the rest of the City in 1642.

PART I

KENSINGTON GARDENS

KENSINGTON GARDENS

I

TOY SOLDIERS AND space men! Once they were Soldiers of the King, set out in their lines ready to scale a stockade, as once they had been Soldiers of the Queen firing at the Turks; now in place of these leaden figures have come moon-struck aviators whose plastic bodies are as leaves before the wind.

Along the paths flanking the eastern (Plate I, facing title-page) and southern walls of Kensington Palace, there is always a moving stream of children: those who have cut down, unchaperoned, from Bayswater with their nets and jars for tiddlers, and those who have been hustled in from Church Street with their hoops and scooters, hurried past York House and, only after a careful glance each way, been allowed free to flit across the Drive and Green of Palace Gardens. The Green was referred to as 'The Moor' as late as the Eighteenth Century, when the Royal Standard would be hoisted daily to show the Court resided there, and the Drive was later called 'Millionaires' Row'. Yet how the names date! The moor has become good grazing ground, a pastoral 'peep' for those retired to Grace and Favour, while the millionaires with their retinues have all departed: in their stead have driven up Buicks with ambassadors and huge foreign staffs. No. 2 Palace Gardens, which was Thackeray's 'last town home', was converted into an R.A.S.C. Headquarters in 1940; today it is the Israeli Embassy. At the far end, from Notting Hill, flies the Russian flag.

Every park has its own social gradings, emphasized by its lie in the land. For so long Kensington has sheltered officers' widows, sisters and daughters that they have become known to the mortuary men at St. Mary Abbot's Hospital as the three Ps.—the Proud; the Poor; and the Patrician. Nor are they easily vanquished, these old ladies who can remember trees being felled to be converted into stocks for muskets

as readily as they can recall the night in February, 1944, when three of
the Royal Borough's churches were ablaze—Protestant, Anglican and
Catholic. In their walks and morning meetings, they keep alive the
faded sepia smile that hides the shillings which they so regularly set
aside for the gas-meter. Ferrules are shod with rubber to steady their
approach, as with a nervous infection the voices of those on scooters
and fairy cycles are hushed in turn; these veterans of voluminous black
command as their fathers, brothers and loved ones did at Gallipoli or
Ladysmith. Here, too, the children are less noisy—their games subdued
to the grey and blue of their blazers, not gashed with the crimson and
purple of the back streets, a shotsilk of joy and misery; here, down these
avenues, now glide swiftly pedalled limousines, where a fair-haired,
blue-eyed child—idolized by her nurses—used to ride the donkey
which she had been given by her uncle York. But on rainy days when
she played in her nursery, she would repeatedly say to her friend (who
was later to become Lady Jane Ellice), 'You must not touch those toys;
they are mine; and I may call you Jane, but you must not call me
Victoria.' Or when she played with the daughter of Sir John Conroy,
the Duchess's major-domo, they would be followed at a dignified pace
as they scampered across the lawns; yet if her companion could forget
herself in the fun, Victoria could never forget the presence of the
scarlet flunkey who bloomed so suddenly and unexpectedly like a giant
peony behind any bush at the slightest pretext.

Today, facing east—commanding as it seems the Borough of
Westminster (for Kensington stretches no further than the Broad
Walk)—is the Queen carved in carrara marble at the time of her
accession. She is crowned and holds a sceptre, and beneath her feet
there reads an inscription saying that this is the loyal gift of 'her
Kensington subjects . . . to commemorate fifty years of her reign'.
Occasionally I have wondered if Princess Louise when she chipped away
at the figure of her mother ever thought of Sir Gilbert Scott's comment
when he ordered the Prince Consort to be cast in gun-metal for the
Albert Memorial: 'I have chosen the sitting position as best conveying
the idea of dignity befitting a royal personage.'

Until quite recently the Broad Walk was lined with elms: but the
winds blew dangerously, the shallow roots sweated decay, and the

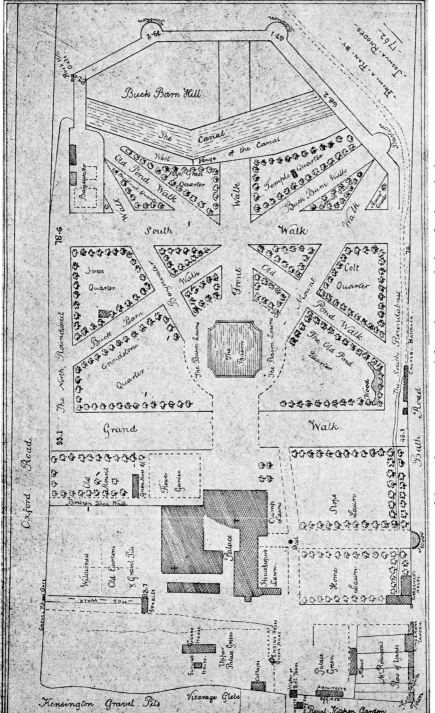

II. A Map of the Gardens in 1764, copied from the original plan of Joshua Rhodes.

The Royal Palace of KINGSINGTON.

III. 'The Royal Palace of Kingsington'; a popular hand-coloured print sold in the reign of William III.

massive girths were condemned to be cut down. New saplings of lime have been planted, protected by chestnut palings against the prying hand or sharp February gust. Another panorama has been altered—though this time the act has not been one of 'unspeakable barbarity'. Under the lash of W. H. Hudson, the Commissioners of Woods and Forests learnt a lesson which they have not forgotten. Here is his lament for the famous rookery of seven hundred trees so savagely destroyed in 1880:

Never grass and trees in their early spring foliage looked so vividly green, while above the sky was clear and blue as if I had left London leagues behind. As I advanced farther into this wooded space the dull sounds of the traffic became fainter, while ahead the continuous noise of cawing rooks grew louder and louder. I was soon under the rookery listening to and watching the birds as they wrangled with one another, and passed in and among the trees or soared above their tops. How intensely black they looked amidst the fresh brilliant green of the sunlit foliage! What wonderfully tall trees were these where the rookery was placed!

Alas! the grove has gone, and the rook is almost a stranger to inner London. So too is the jackdaw which, even in the 'Nineties, was becoming 'far less loquacious and more sedate in manner than daws are wont to be'. A few still nest at the entrance to the Broad Walk and recently nesting-boxes have been put up to induce them to stay.

Up this stretch of mile, fifty foot wide, Bayswater and Queensway lie at the far end. On a snowy day beneath the northern cupolas of the Coburg Court Hotel there is a suggestion of droskis waiting for fares as the whiteness of the sky becomes resolved in the blackness of the railings, which meet at Lion Gate. 'The unkillable infants of the very poor' continue to drag their home-made toboggans here. But turn about with the poet and at the Gloucester Road entrance to the Broad Walk, 'by the railing of a path in Kensington Gardens', walks she who is 'dying piece-meal of a sort of emotional anaemia' and a kind of longing 'for someone to speak to her'—yet

> almost afraid that I
> will commit that indiscretion.

Where Ezra Pound kept silent beneath the shade of his ten-gallon hat, did others make bold? In the last forty years the scene has not varied —only aged: every afternoon, between half-past two and four, an exquisite boredom reigns as of hands hovering between Caroline sauce-boats and the Queen Anne sugar-bowl; those figures blown 'like a skein of loose silk against a wall' are now swathed in pale forget-me-not as they float down these paths with the same ease that first caused a Middle Westerner to thrust out his redly bearded jaw with Aryan determination. Not much missed his fierce nordic eyes as he saw in this parade 'the end of breeding'. Yet his ambiguity does not allow for the real truth which is perhaps that these were the newly disinherited—the mourners of Zeebrugge or Mons and an equerry cut short in the blaze of his career.

Nearly parallel with the Coburg Court Hotel, on the southern boundary of the Park, is the Milestone Hotel, which marks the stop of the old coaches on their way to Hammersmith. Again, by cutting back the trees which used to overhang the road, the Commissioners of Woods and Forests have quite literally taken a piece of natural history out of the hands of Londoners; but they have done so with the help of the Transport Board.

When the horse-drawn omnibuses used to rumble along and stop at the Milestone or the Broad Walk, hands on the upper deck would greedily snatch at a twig to take to the City; and the chances were more than likely that their act would be met with the cries of nuthatch and reed-warbler, cuckoo or nightingale. Then, through the dusty summers, these green tokens lying on desks would give promise of a world glimpsed beyond the letters of plaintiffs or deeds of covenant so labouriously copied through the day and sometimes brought home in brief-cases whose empty cheeks would collapse like those of a starved man. Here was a legacy of Mayhew, with industry's ivy of smoke which in time was to soot even the trees of the Park so that the familiar bird-cries grew practically extinct and in their place were heard the new cries of blackbird and robin, blue-tit and thrush.

'The way to see London is from the top of a 'bus—the top of a 'bus, gentlemen.' Gladstone's voice, with its punctilious correctitude, has the ring of the public meeting; but it was addressed to a small band of American visitors. Yet despite his passion for reform—reform in education; reform in the Church; reform in parliamentary elections—he never breathed a word about those kind ladies who later would ask passengers, 'Are you saved?' or who, a little later still, grew bold enough to distribute papers with the exhaltation in heavy Gothic type to 'Vote for Women'. *Plus ça change plus c'est la même chose.* Yet now that the top decks are covered in, they have become as dangerous as the lower. This Kensington fare-stage, with its 73 route bound for Marble Arch, still carries its female warriors and, even if they are less amazonian and vocal than their predecessors, the Gothic print prevails. 'How Would You Like To Be Vivisected?' ask their leaflets. Or, 'Outlaw the H-Bomb', I once heard a man shout as the bus passed the Albert Hall.

Is it the casual cuckoo with his narrow, pointed wings, or is it the evocation of the name Flower Walk, which conjures for this corner of the Park a perpetual association with summer? Certainly, when winter comes, the surrounding windswept paths are to be hurried down, just as the stage coaches, with mud to the blinkers, would hurry down the flanking stretch of lane. But the ruts which bred such a general infection of ill temper have been macadamized and now this road is no more than a link between men's homes and their work, a highway whose depressing endless stucco is as impersonal as the black burrows through which the trains rattle from Kensington to Hyde Park. Only in the spring, when the first crocus pierces the green slopes, do motorists slow their pace and take the South Carriage Drive which, together with its western and northern extensions, rings Hyde Park in one.[1] All along this Kensington Gore boundary there is a landscape gardening that needs heat to bring it alive; for behind the outer shallow hilly mounds, which edge the street, lies the more formal Flower Walk—or Babies Walk as it is sometimes called.

Good landscape gardening demands a talent similar to generalship, and it may be no mere coincidence that billets in barracks are so often surrounded by geraniums, set out in formal lines, and paraded before rows of white-blancoed markers.

For different Kensington gardeners under different queens, not wishing to be press-ganged into military service, have almost accidentally put into their well-disciplined herbaceous borders and avenues of trees something of that soldier's bearing which their own bent bodies

[1] There is a speed limit of 20 m.p.h.

have so sadly lacked. On hot Sunday afternoons when the Grenadiers
play and the resounding clash of cymbals quivers the air, there is an
anticipated regularity about their choice of favourites: 'Goodbye,
Dolly Grey', medleys from *No, No, Nannette!*, or

> There is something about a soldier,
> Something about a soldier,
> Something about a soldier
> That is fine, fine, fine.
> He may be a sergeant-major. . . .

It is ironical on such afternoons to stir the memory and recall the
Archbishop of Canterbury who a century ago had a military band[1]
silenced on this site, or the parliamentarians who agitated to have a
penalty imposed upon all bishops and clergy who drove or rode to
church. For, between waking and dozing, what a strange reasoning
relates the hoof of horse with the poised drumstick and the Lord's peace.
Or, on such afternoons, what curious parables of light fall when the
leaves hide the Royal Standard flying from the Palace and the June-
roses are in full petal. By the June-rose, poets have celebrated their
countryside at a level profounder than any set of verses about the
Colours. Indeed, it should never be forgotten that the poster-artists
who drew England as a garden of flowers, or who separated the rose
from the rest, fostered morale in wartime canteens in a way which
must have been as much a surprise to enemy agents as it still appears to
be to a number of statesmen in the present House.[2]

Somewhat in this vein, 'Wise and Loudon [the landscape gardeners]
are our heroic poets', began Addison in Number 477 of *The Spectator*,
and then continued:

and if, as critic, I may single out any passage of their works to commend,
I shall take notice of that part in the upper garden at Kensington [i.e. half a
mile north of today's Flower Walk], which at first was nothing but a gravel-
pit. It must have been a fine genius for gardening that could have thought of
forming such an unsightly hollow into so beautiful an area, and to have hit
the eye with so uncommon and agreeable a scene as that which it is now
wrought into. To give this particular spot of ground the greater effect, they
have made a very pleasing contrast; for, as on one side of the walk you see

[1] Bands at present play every afternoon from May to September.
[2] Readers are referred to *Hansard* and some of the comments made in debate about
similar poster campaigns for National Savings, National Sweepstakes, etc., etc.

24

this hollow basin, with its several little plantations laying conveniently under the eye of the beholder, on the other side of it there appears a seeming mount, made up of trees, rising one higher than another, in proportion as they approach the centre.

Haydon also in his *Autobiography* speaks of Kensington's 'most poetical bits of tree and stump, and sunny brown and green glens and tawny earth', whilst at different times various rumours have had it that trees have been planted in battle-formations—as at Blenheim or Waterloo; but no evidence can be found to corroborate such stories.

The paradox by which Kensington's *gardens* are classified among London's four central *parks* provides an example of history in a nutshell. Originally there were *laid-out gardens* and *open parkland*; both were quite distinct, as indeed they were in 1690 when the King chanced to hear that there were two country houses for sale westward of London, one on the road to Kensington, the other beyond that village. William III did not buy Holland House, or Cope's Castle as it was locally known, but he did buy Nottingham House from the Lord Chancellor Heneage Finch. 'Old Dismal' his contemporaries would toast him in their glasses—and even though he was

> At the bar abusive, on the bench unable,
> Knave at the woolsack, fop at the council-table—

at least in business he seems to have remained remarkably astute. The sale included twenty-six acres and the sum demanded was £18,000. Evelyn in his diaries describes the property as 'a patched up building *with gardens*'. The King wanted his new Palace to be within easy reach of the offices of his government, and the dryness of the air from the nearby sand-pits was ideal for an asthmatic (Plate II, facing p. 20). Further, so as to keep his royal messengers in close contact with Whitehall and Westminster, he had a high road cut through the well-timbered forest adjoining his Gardens and continued through Hyde Park, Green Park and St. James's. During the winter it was lit with three hundred lanthorns—the first illuminated highway of its kind and hence winning from the engravers the epithets of 'very grand' and 'inconceivably magnificent'; in the summer, the lamps were kept at the Palace woodyard until such time as they would be needed for 'their Majesties' further service'.

The improvement of his estate became the King's passion. Wren was summoned to add another floor to Nottingham House. Within a year £60,000 had been spent, but on the 10th November, 1691, a fire broke out and their Majesties only just escaped being burnt in their beds. As they stood beside the clipped dragons of yew and the box-tree grenadiers, so their Footguards passed bucket from hand to hand until all the flames had been extinguished. *Dum Vivo Lucio.* The fire was as good an excuse as any for a new suite of rooms and a new south front; Wren was summoned a second time. Eleven years later the King when riding his sorrel pony near Hampton Court was badly thrown. He begged to be brought back to Kensington to die.

Queen Anne on her accession enlarged his Dutch Gardens, visiting the Palace every year for an Easter recess to which the world of society flocked 'in brocaded robes, hoops, fly-caps, and fans'. Her love of flowers made Tom D'Urfey apostrophize her in a ballad as 'Great Flora'. She had thirty acres taken off the Parkland adjoining old Nottingham House and added to the Gardens of her Palace, ordering as well a fosse and wall to be made to mark the new boundary. In early maps and deeds, this is referred to as the 'Ha Ha'—an onomato-poeic word meant to suggest the cries of townsfolk as they venture thus far out and find that they can go no further (Plate VII, facing p. 37).

Queen Caroline, too, concentrated on increasing the Parkland, while the King decided to make the Gardens less formal. (George II believed that the money she spent was her own and it was not until her death that he discovered that Walpole had granted her over £20,000 from the royal revenue.) The plan of the Gardens at the time of William III had been 'the Siege of Troy' (Plate III, facing p. 21); the clipped hedges were meant to represent fortifications; figuratively, the notion that his palace was also his castle pleased the Dutch sovereign. But the new King favoured a more domestic arrangement; an Englishman's home was not a castle—home was where the heart is; he would have the strict symmetry broken down by curves, just as his Queen rebelled against the ornamental waters of the period which were either rectangular or square (Plates II and V, facing pp. 20 and 29). Yet her rebellion was only half successful. She had the Round Pond sunk, and she employed Charles Withers to join the pools of Hyde Park with the

West Bourne brook and thus make an artificial lake which should be serpentine. She kept to her name, even though her architect failed to keep to his contract. The Serpentine covers nearly forty acres, but has only one curve (Plates X and XI, facing pp. 42 and 43).

At one time the Doge of Genoa sent her a large number of tortoises; these she introduced with a number of red-squirrels to the Park. The tortoises died out, but the squirrels continued to populate the groves until early this century an epidemic struck the species, which was fatal. Again, up until early this century, deer were kept, and in a minute from the Board of Green Cloth, dated 1798, it is reported that foxes were hunted. Another minute also records a pension of £18 a year to Sarah Grey 'in compassion for the loss of her husband, who had been accidentally shot by one of the keepers'. Hunting consequently features in many prints of the Park. In the forefront, ladies are seen strolling in avenues, while spaniels snap at the ribbons of their hats slung upon their arms. Then, like a bubble in the mind, in a far corner a chase is in full pursuit; but if the bubble is pricked—Who smiles on Who? Does my Lady's dimple come for my Lord who short of breath is already back in the field, or for he who has followed the master's horn and is ready for the kill? These Eighteenth Century prints teach a reader to be patient with the historian who must untie the knots of Augustan heredity.

When the Court moved to Richmond in the 1790s, the Gardens and Park were thrown open on Sundays to all save sailors, soldiers and liveried servants.[1] (Did the gardeners still fear the recruiting sergeant?)

---

[1] This 'favouritism', as it was called, brought forth much abuse, and it became a pastime of servants to band together and mock those who entered the Gardens. One irate protest to the press came from a gentleman who signed himself 'Reformer': it was published in the *Morning Herald*:

Your paper being circulated in the moſt polite part of the Town, I beg leave, through the channel thereof, to recommend to the ladies and gentlemen who viſit Kenſington Gardens on Sunday, to give notice to their ſervants that they behave themselves decently. Yeſterday it was hardly poſſible to get near the gate leading into the Gardens, for the croud of ſervants who gathered round there, and who inſulted every person not particularly known to them, going in, or coming out of the Gardens. Unfortunately for my ſervant, I found him one of thoſe gentry, and have already discharged him, and if the like is practiſed on any future day when I am preſent, I shall take the liberty of giving the diſcipline of the horſewhip to ſuch as I may catch purſuing the like line of conduct, and that I may not be under the neceſſity of doing ſo, beg you will give them notice thereof by inſerting this.

A strict formality of dress was demanded: no one wearing a silken necktie or breeches without boots was admitted—'nor indeed anyone whose appearance the gatekeepers did not consider respectable'. I quote from Surtees whose next sentence contains the sting: 'None of the great unwashed were to be seen in the Park in those days.'

In the next century, the Gardens were kept open from spring to autumn (Plate IX, facing p. 39), and sometimes by the Round Pond Shelley would be seen sailing paper yachts. One legend has it that they were made of five pound notes. (Harriet Westbrook, his first wife, drowned herself in the Serpentine in 1816.) Then, early in Victoria's reign, the Park was 'opened all the year round, to all respectably dressed persons'. New gravel paths were laid, and as it was to Kensington's 'unpolluted air' that William III had retired, so now repaired 'Gloriana's dames of Britain'. As Tickell closes his set of verses:

> Here while the town in damp and darkness lies
> They breathe in sunshine and see azure skies;
> Each walk with robes of various dyes bespread,
> Seen from afar a moving tulip bed.

Time had let burgeon in these Gardens of Kensington and its Park a splendid naturalness. That is a turn of phrase with an Eighteenth Century undertone, but it was echoed over and over by Nineteenth Century traveller after traveller. 'Like a good mile of the Forest of St. Germain in the heart of town', declared one French visitor. Or as Disraeli would dramatize—'The forests of Spenser and Aristo'. What had been the delight of royalty had become the property of the people; the Park had not been made for them, but given to them as by a 'Faery Queen'. Lord Beaconsfield was bowing very low; and pointing to the open carriage door (he despised the horse-omnibus), he would say: 'In exactly ten minutes it is in the power of every man to free himself from the tumult of the world'. Another Prime Minister before him had called the parks 'the lungs of London'. He would only add: 'God Bless her Majesty!'

IV. Kensington Palace from the South; a popular hand-coloured print sold at the Black Horse in Cornhill.

V. 'Veue du Palais du Coté de L'Orient'; a print designed by John Rocque for sale at the Sugar Loaf & Cannister in Great Windmill Street.

II

T HE EYE NEEDS its own darkroom to develop what it sees, and this is particularly true with park statuary. The carrara marble that Princess Louise worked achieves an inner luminosity when it is remembered rather than seen; the statue of William III with his long hair, plumed hat and knee-boots becomes magnified in retrospect. By day the plush green sward and the clipped yew hedges dissolve into the jade-red brickfront of Wren's Palace (I had intended writing faded-red, but my pen slipped—and to happy advantage; for distance blurs the lawn into a rose-red emphasizing the furze of moss which is slowly creeping up towards the sills.) Yet at home it is Herr Bancke's double life size figure which stays in the mind, that gift of a namesake, William II, the last German Emperor and King of Prussia, who presented it to 'Edward VII for the British Nation'. But it is late summer light that snaps in the bronze cheeks the William whose Mary awoke such devoted love that when she lay in a deep lethargy, so well did the King stifle his asthma, that she called out to her gentlewoman, 'Where is my Sovereign, for I do not hear him cough?' This is the perfect setting for the Dutch monarch—and August offers the perfect time-exposure.

For the Albert Memorial late autumn is the perfect setting, and early morning the time for the best exposure. Passing No. 5 Hyde Park Place, at which Dickens resided for a period, the profile of Albert of Saxe-Coburg-Gotha comes into focus, facing his own Memorial Hall—for which, after the erection of his own colossal shrine,[1] insufficient money remained from public subscription until eventually a joint-stock company built it as a business venture.[2] Moreover at this

[1] It cost £120,000.

[2] The actual building was done by Messrs. Lucas Bros., who had already shown at the Royal Albert Docks and Liverpool Street Station that they were capable of a bold and imaginative use of cast iron. The Hall stands on the site of Gore House, the famous residence of Lady Blessington from 1836-49.

hour, early in the morning, when the leaves begin to fall there is something superbly Gothic and theatrical about the effect—as if they would whisper with Nicholas Nickleby, 'all are alike, but here there is none like me'. Papering the ground, they seem nature's immortelles for a Prince Regent respected, venerated, admired—yet never quite taken to the heart of his adopted people. There is in the downward drift of dark foliage just the slightest hint of histrionic rather than historic obsequies, as at a transformation scene. For suddenly Victoria is widowed, the branches deep black.

Yet any moment snow may descend and alter everything. Then, as the flakes begin to fall softly, so the tremendous figures of Faith, Hope and Charity become shrouded with those of Astronomy, Chemistry and Geometry, Rhetoric, Medicine and Philosophy: grouped beneath the massive pillars of Cornish granite are four tableaux—with a bull symbolizing Europe, a camel Africa, a bison America, and an elephant Asia. These now might be the floats for a glorious wedding-cake finale to an English durbar. Months have gone to its preparation, years to its planning. She who plays Physiology carries on her left arm an infant so that she may bear witness that she holds 'the highest and most perfect of physiological forms'. Her finger points to an instrument, the better to suggest the march of science, for the instrument is a microscope which 'lends its assistance for the investigation of the minuter forms of animal and vegetable organisms'. And in all this dumbstruck magnificence lies a truth—as though to say no longer shall mankind paint like the barbarian or harlot, but from child to elder all shall be innocent alike. This is Lapland come to London through a penny peepshow! Yet with the years, these fantasies fade. . . .

'It is God reading the Bible.' A child is speaking. Certainly others have thought that the book which Prince Albert holds is the Bible; in actual fact, in the words of Mr. J. H. Foley, the sculptor, it is 'a catalogue of [the Great Exhibition of 1851]—that first gathering of the industry of all nations'. Yet the figurehead of a fifteen foot high Godhead was never far from Sir Gilbert Scott's original conception: 'My idea in designing the Memorial was to erect a kind of ciborium to protect a statue of the Prince', and moreover 'its special characteristic was that this ciborium was designed in some degree on the principles of the ancient shrines'. As he went on to elaborate: 'These shrines are models of imaginary buildings such as had never in reality been erected; and my idea was to realize one of these imaginary structures with its precious metals, its inlayings, its enamels etc., etc. . . .'

In 1864 work had begun; twelve years later it was completed (Plate XII, facing p. 44). During the building, several dinners were given for the workmen and upwards of eighty sat at the tables constructed of scaffold planks. Beef, mutton, plum-pudding and cheese were served; also ale—though a large proportion were teetotallers who kept to lemonade or ginger beer. As the architect describes one dinner: 'several toasts were given and many of the workmen spoke, almost all of them commencing by "Thanking God that they enjoyed good health" ', and alluding to the temperance that prevailed among them and 'how little swearing was heard'.

Did the awe 'of being engaged upon so great a work' create a false aura of respect?—that is a question raised by lampoonists at the time, which is still relevant. For recently when the statuary was cleaned it was found that caricatures had been scratched on the backs of many of the heads. Were these the revenges of time, the joke haloes of sober awe? In a hundred years or less who would distinguish between Pugin, Barry and Cockerell or Cheops, Hiram and Sennacherib?[1] The years of building had not been popular years for the Queen; in 1872 a youth of seventeen tried to assassinate her outside Buckingham Palace and the broadsheets had been full of malicious gossip. Yet within just over a decade such irreparable losses had followed—first Princess Alice, then Lord Beaconsfield, John Brown and Prince Leopold—that as new weeds were added and her body moved more slowly, supported by a stick, so public sympathy enfolded the Queen ever more closely. Her love of obelisks, pyramids and seats of inscribed granite became national marks of mourning. Prince Francis Charles Augustus Albert Emanuel achieved a popularity which he had never known during his life; his image was made immortal all over the country—in Perth, in Wolverhampton and in Aberdeen as well as in Holborn, Kensington

[1] In all there are one hundred and seventy-eight figures: they are the work of H. H. Armstead and J. B. Philip.

31

and outside the Licensed Victuallers' Asylum in the Old Kent Road; delayed suspicion had turned to lasting trust.

The Queen profoundly distrusted George Frederick Watts. It is an odd perversity that the park authorities should have allowed his famous statue of Physical Energy to be planted a few hundred yards behind her Albert Memorial. The title is well chosen, for to this replica of the central section of the Rhodes Memorial at Table Mountain, the London climate has brought its own modifications. In Cape Town, in the full blaze of the sun with no shadows to cast doubts, the horsed rider is Energy Exalted; in Lancaster Walk, even on the hottest day, grey streaks left by birds make their own commentary on the black curls. It is as if Swinburne's chariot hurries near, as its four steeds pull at their reins in praise of the sculptor's eightieth birthday:

> And Love, by life made sad and glad,
> Gave Conscience ease, and watched Good-Will pass by.
> All these make music now on one man's name,
> Whose life and age are one with love and fame.

In 1921 when the now defunct *John o' London's Weekly* asked its readers to vote for the most beautiful statue in London, with nearly one accord, they all chose Peter Pan. The runner-up was Richard I. Neither Physical Energy nor the Albert Memorial were within the first twenty.

Sir George Frampton's figure had been unveiled nine years before, and on the latter's tomb in St. Paul's there is a cast of a child holding a replica of the Park's statue. Yet even in so authoritative a work as William Kent's *Encyclopaedia of London*, nowhere in the article on 'Kensington Gardens'[1] is Peter Pan listed—though J. H. Speke's obelisk and Sir Edward Jenner's[2] bronze both feature. The reason for this omission may be the fact that a good many Londoners regard Peter Pan not as a statue but a monument, and in my childhood, when two vandals crept in and tarred and feathered it, the outcry in the papers lasted a full nine days. Some have argued that its constant

[1] This omission in the article in question is redeemed later in the article on 'Statues' —although the inconsistency remains significant.

[2] The discoverer of vaccination, who, as a subscriber to Leigh Hunt's *Juvenilia* in 1804, is described as 'the author of the most ingenious discovery of the eighteenth century'.

popularity is due to a desire to remain young, to assert as English audiences so loudly do each year that they still believe in fairies. Perhaps, so the argument is maintained, it is just one of those traditional oddities like a man playing a part of the Dame in pantomime, or officers waiting upon other ranks at Christmas. Or again, others have suggested that its popularity reflects a kind of arrested development on a national scale,[1] whilst others go on to further this argument by calling in the mass-observers who explain that at any rate the average mental age is thirteen. . . .

So here instead I am going to try and drain away the sediment of the years and see the statue as I first saw it. I have my eyes closed and what I recall most clearly is moss gripping the edges of the crazy paving stones as I myself grip at the rabbit whose ears have been smoothed by the stroking of a thousand similar small hands. Out of the bronze trunk emerge other figures whose bodies curl upwards like wisps of smoke. But 'Peter Pan, Peter Pan', I can hear my own voice cry as I hold a sustained note that is neither of pain nor pleasure: 'Where is Peter Pan?'

Suddenly my feet no longer touch the ground. I am being lifted up and yet as I become airborne I have no desire to look. The impression I remember is of a Peter who flew, a Peter who defied Captain Hook, a Peter whose house with Wendy in the tree tops only disappeared when a heavy plush curtain hid the scene from sight.

The actors of the year, as I have checked, were Jean Forbes-Robertson and the late Sir Gerald du Maurier. I sometimes think of the dramatic critic who a few seasons back wrote of an actress: 'If this Peter Pan entered my nursery, I would dial 999.' Possibly for the children of that year Frampton's shepherd boy with his pipe and smock will remain the reality. Or perhaps, thirty years from now, I shall meet myself in the old men who shuffle along this embankment complaining that Barrie robbed Pan to play Peter by making a beautiful neuter out of a centaur who, 'hairy all over should have been half man and half beast'. Yet perhaps forty years hence I shall be resigned. 'To live long is to change

---

[1] Wyndham Lewis represents many when he comments: 'The sickly and dismal spirit of that terrible key-book, Peter Pan, has sunk into every tissue of the social life in England.'

often,' said Newman. Looking at the bolder mallards as they cross from the Serpentine and peck at the crazy paving, I think of Blake standing on the other side during one of his morning walks: 'The man who never alters his opinion is like standing water, and breeds reptiles of the mind.'

III

ON THE OPEN strips of grass at the feet of the marble Queen, that border the western shores of the Round Pond, small figures gyrate and stagger; invisible skeins connect them to the sky as far away tiny specks of white pull against the gravity of the earth. This is a falling arc from blue to green—a descent from a metaphysic as free as the air to one bounded by the trees and hillocks. A happy-go-lucky network of string surrounds the models of both ocean liner and tea-clipper as they lie dry-docked on the asphalt. But at twelve noon on Sundays the starters are ready with their flags, the time-keepers with their stop-watches. The Round Pond becomes a Solent with Southampton Waters adjoining.

As the sails belly out and catch the prevailing wind, so all the mathematical precision of these racing yachts makes a tub of the small boat that drifts idly in their wake. For a brief hour this might be a dress-rehearsal for a Cowes regatta, while across the water on another shore, marked out by buoys, funnels belch smoke. Hooters and sirens lend to the slipway here all the imaginary excitement of hauser and crane. As the H.M.S. *Implacable* steams off on her course, so undisturbed the grebes and moorhens swim past at gun-level.

Every day too, but more especially on Sundays, the gulls wait to be fed.[1] Small grease-proof bags with a week's rind and crusts are religiously brought and, as a cast of seed flung into the air will bring a flight of birds together on a patch of field, so it is the same with the gulls as they fly up with their red beaks open and then descend once more in a close flock, sitting high on the water, facing the wind, waiting for the next bagful. Cockneys are apt to forget that their city is also a seaport; but in Salford offices, Mancunians do not: postscripts in business letters speak of a good week's fishing spent by cotton kings

[1] 'In a very cheerful mood. Pleased with myself and everybody till a seagull soared overhead in Kensington Gardens and aroused my vast capacities for envy—I wish I could fly.' W. N. P. Barbellion in his *Journal of a Disappointed Man* (10th May, 1914).

of the last century when a day's catch from the Thames might bring together soles, plaice, halibut, haddock and turbot. Today, standing on this higher ridge, a tang of salt in the air tells that the tide is returning up the estuary.

'The birds enjoy a treat.' I catch the familiar Bradford accent. If the parks were royal preserves, so have they always been bird preserves; and the gull has come to take the place of the mediaeval kite or raven as a scavenger. Hudson dates the change-over partly to the bitter winter of 1892-3 when 'hundreds of working men and boys would take advantage of their free hour at dinner time to . . . give the scraps left over from their meals to the birds'. The habit has since grown more and more widespread, and I think that I heard it most poignantly explained by an old nurse who—if I report her correctly—said: 'Men work for six days a week to feed themselves. It is right on the seventh they should feed others.' So it is that eavesdropping, poetry is sometimes heard from those to whom Milton and Keats are names and to whom a mention of Clare or Edward Thomas would only suggest children of another family.

In the warmer months there are two main hours of exodus from the Round Pond on Sundays; the first just before one, the other before tea. Those that stay have either brought picnic baskets, or paper carriers. The picnic baskets troop south towards St. Govor's Well,[1] where the grass is plushy with the promise of strawberries and cream, while the other contingent, looked after by an elder sister, sits on the more northern gravelly soil, which has about its bald patches in summer months an unquenchable thirst for fizzy lemonade. This is a division between rich and poor—though there are trespassers on both sides. Yet to realize how strict this division was at the turn of the century, hear James Barrie speak: 'Quite common children also picnic [on this spot], and the blossom falls into their mugs just the same.' None is ever so snobbish as the self-made man.

Over each camp, the birds wheel and circle. Sometimes after a party

[1] This Well has been buried in. A drinking fountain, east of where Broad Walk begins, marks the place. A plaque now reads: 'This Drinking Fountain errected in 1951 marks the site of an Ancient Spring which in 1856 was named St. Govor's Well after the Patron Saint of Llanover by Sir Benjamin Hall First Commissioner of Works 1855-58 created Lord Llanover in 1859.'

VI. Haymaking in the Gardens, c. 1777; a water-colour by Thomas Hearne.

VII. The Ha Ha on the Eastern Boundary; a wash-drawing by A. B. Lens, 1736.

has packed up its rugs, folded up its deck chairs and shaken out its crumbs, the noise of beaks tapping the hard soil or path is like what countrymen call 'pigeon hail'. In the 1730s when a flock of geese migrated from St. James's Park to Kensington and there scratched and pecked holes in the gravel paths, Lord Essex who was Keeper to the Royal House, with the stern justice of a Draco, ordered the offending geese to be shot. Such military spirit earned him a captaincy in the Yeomen of the Guard in 1739.

Today the geese have their own retreats by the Serpentine. The pigeons however, though frequent visitors, seldom perch in the trees and still less seldom do they nest there; they prefer parapets or ledges to branches, thereby showing their natural descent from rock-doves who breed in either crags or crevices. They are also slowly losing the white in their plumage—another reminder of their rock ancestry.

As the evening begins to draw in, the paths that lead to the different gates assume an impenetrable hardness; it is as if beneath their crust they had trapped the cut knees and grazed hands of countless boys and girls. 'Do not make light of the troubles of the young,' W. B. Yeats's uncle was fond of repeating at the dinner-table: 'They can be worse than ours, because we can see the end of our troubles and they can never see the end.' Of all nightmares, those behind the bars of the cot can often be the worst: at this stage, and later in the kindergarten, nursery or sandpit, an earthquake can still be compared to a skin of milk trembling before it boils. So far there is no knowledge of that reality of which geologists speak when they refer to the world as a ball of fire whose crust alone is hard. Again, if the truth of philosophers and mystics achieve a milky whiteness, this is frequently put down to senile decay or second childhood. To dismiss such censure as the brashness or impertinence of youth is to forget how much easier it is to be agnostic at twenty than eighty-one. For truths have a habit of unrolling like mottoes from crackers on just those occasions when so often three generations of a family meet under one roof.

> What are heavy? sea-sand and sorrow:
> What are brief? today and tomorrow:
> What are frail? spring blossoms and youth:
> What are deep? the ocean and truth.

A week ago when I was walking in Kensington I knew that I should mention the gravelly soil near the Round Pond's Bayswater shore; I knew also that I should quote a passage from Dame Julian of Norwich, which I have always associated with this side of the Gardens. Only now when I come to copy it out does my eye catch a biographical note and I read that her home 'was most begrowing with seaweed and gravel'. Here is the text, from the fifth chapter of the first of her *Revelations*:

In this time our Lord showed me a spiritual sight of His homely loving. . . .

Also in this He showed me a little thing, the quantity of a hazel-nut, in the palm of my hand; and it was as round as a ball. I looked thereupon with eye of my understanding and thought: *What may this be?* And it was answered generally thus: *It is all that is made.* . . .

Sea-sand, a hazel-nut, and spring blossoms—they are the symbols by which poets and mystics communicate their vision: they are the signs which explain other signs and that philosophers interpret. To lakes, rivers and ponds everybody brings what he sees there—even the birds; to each his own reflection as it were. Such perhaps is the metaphysic of the park and its water-gazers.

North-east of the Round Pond stands the Elfin Oak of Ivor Innes. From this half body of a tree, an owl stares down—not Shakespeare's 'fatal bellman', but a bird whose beak pressages a mortar-board and cane. If the chiseller has kept the grey close-cropped feathers from spreading into a black gown, there yet remains trapped in the wood all the untutored fears of the young when they invest in certain of their teachers the terror of a tiger, the eye of a hawk—or when a scout, posted at the door to keep *cave*, will signal silence to a whole class by the one word 'beak'. But here the order has been reversed. This is the animal kingdom carved with human attributes—a sort of protracted infantilism. It is noticeable that the gnomes of Innes are not dwarfs but little men; their red and green pixie caps emphasize their stunted features—and this perhaps more than anything else dates the oak, for it was set up in 1928. Yet if in the late 'Twenties Barrie's whimsy was on the wane, a return to pre-Raphaelite golden lords and ladies found no more favour than a return to the knights and dragons of Arthurian myth: instead there was abroad then a social ethic whose elfin ethic

Interior

VIII. The Queen Anne Engine House on the Western Boundary; a water-colour
by an unknown Eighteenth Century Artist.

IX. Kensington Gardens Summer Walking Dress; a print from the *Weekly Messenger*, 11th June, 1806.

was likewise infected with a desire to replace the supernatural by the natural, to make of a gnome or pixie no more than a stunted little man.

Has the novelty of pixies cut from gnarled wood died? Have the ashtrays from Birmingham bred a familiarity of contempt for gnomes? Nowadays, at this corner of the Children's Playground, only rarely does a freckled face press itself against the iron fence that keeps the beckoning figures just beyond arm's reach. Then a shout from the sand-pit or swings or tall grass and Elfin Oak is deserted once more.

'In a cowslip's bell I lie.' The constant tramp of feet at this Bayswater boundary of the Park means that few flowering plants survive in the meadow or rye grass—though wall-barley and patches of cocksfoot thrive. Occasionally large tracts are roped off while new seed is left to grow. Once, too, along the edges of these paths fences were set at right angles at fixed intervals. This was to prevent children from wearing away the outskirts of the swards. George Lansbury however had them taken away—and so it is possible again to catch 'the forest-like glades of Kensington' which the illustrators of Jorrocks' England captured. Thither Tittlebat Titmouse would come for a quiet walk (in Hyde Park he would have 'promenaded'), and for 'a penny or twopenny seat'[1] he would discover that he could watch, if not converse, 'with the aristocracy of England', since the Gardens had then, as they yet retain, a preserved exclusiveness about them. Matthew Arnold's lines can still be read in their natural setting:

> In this lone, open glade I lie,
>   Screened by deep boughs on either hand;
> And at its end, to stay the eye,
>   Those black-crown'd, red-boled pine trees stand.

Again, like Tittlebat Titmouse in *Ten Thousand a Year* who would come to ape gentlemen, so others can still be seen acting similarly—though with differently placed accents on their performances. Once boys would call 'beaver' after old gentlemen with beards and run for

---

[1] A history has yet to be written about park seats and benches—although there is perhaps one observation to be made in passing. Invariably they all face the paths. Can it be that this factor has made one London suburb see that its benches on one side of its Green face, not the flowers and grass, but the railway line?

it; later it was just a case of asking the time in the hope of seeing half-hunters snap open; now, without blushing, it is a test of asking lovers in deck chairs the way to the Flower Walk or the Orangery.

On a blustery day in February, Queen Anne's Orangery provides shelter against rain and wind (just visible behind the Palace in Plate IV, facing p. 28); it lies within two minutes of the Children's Playground. Facing the familiar red-brick of Wren and the green slatted roof is the Sunken Garden with its terraced formality, its pleached lime walk and three leaden tanks; an oblong stretch cut into the centre makes a pool for lilies. I remember seeing a production of *Cinderella* with a scene called 'The Magic Pool' which had been fitted in to show off the wonderful stage effects that could be achieved at the Theatre Royal, Drury Lane. Sixteen nymphs descended one behind the other, their arms stretched up and fingers touching—yet so controlled in their movement that, as they sank out of sight, scarcely a bubble told of their disappearance; then a few seconds later, a hand rose bearing the glass slipper. Well might this garden inherited by 'Great Flora' inspire such a scene, for there is in the constant overflow of water from the leaden tanks a rhythm so perfect that it creates its own musical figures of sound. This is music made visible—the right key for Thomas Augustine Arne who, born four years before the Queen's death in 1714, was within fifty to be chief 'musical composer' at Drury Lane.

The hawthorn trees that she had planted in rows between her Orangery and this Sunken Garden suggest so well those fragrant airs of his. No struggles of the soul, no fine frenzies of passion—just formal avenues of song. Contemporaries said that he was the rival of Handel, which is rather like saying that the Round Pond is the rival of the Serpentine: both contain water as both composers gave a certain watery texture to their work—yet there the comparison must end. Dr. Arne knew his limits; the oratorio for a hundred voices was not for him. He wanted the small platform of the Pleasure Gardens at Vauxhall, or the steps of the Orangery at Kensington. There, his talent could reign supreme; and there might Mrs. Arne sing his songs—as beaux and belles whistling his tunes, humming his melodies, would send them like an invisible pollen into every shire throughout the land.

To remember his setting for 'Blow, Blow thou winter wind' or

'Where the bee sucks', and to stand between the bays and may trees that divide the Orangery from the pleached lime walk, is to know a peak moment of the Eighteenth Century—a moment hovering between the sculptured excellence of Gibbons' festoons which Wren chose and the boast of a Prime Minister that coarse conversation was the only talk that everybody could enjoy, or a century that could applaud the hanging of a thief at ten wearing a pinafore with the same admiration that it would applaud the stamina of Fox who after eighteen hours at the tables rose to deliver the most brilliant speech on American taxation that the House has ever heard. Had Blake been widely read then, he would have been wildly suspect. A gentleman, it was assumed, could jog along very nicely on £40,000 a year. Art was no more than an appendage to life—like hunting or bishops. Dr. Arne in his velvet suit never struck a note wrong; his musical pieces and settings had the precision and graceful phrasing so universally admired, praised and cherished. No wonder that he never wanted. He could orchestrate splendidly for the winter wind, even if he could not appreciate its full ingratitude. But then he never had to.

If his ghost ever walks these parts, I wonder what he thinks of the old men who, driven from their rooms, cough their existence out in corners of the Orangery, which from autumn to spring becomes a glorified boarding house of winter hibernation. Withered are all the rare exotic plants that Queen Anne used to keep. Or do the doctor's features become closer pinched as he listens to the mother's-helps who gather each morning while their charges hide in the alcoves behind the Corinthian pilasters? Here, Queen Anne 'sometimes counsel took, sometimes tay'; but now all that is taken is shelter or a sleep—and sometimes a handbag.

Augustus Hare in his walks through Kensington constantly takes William Kent, the Yorkshire landscape gardener and painter, to task. 'Much spoilt by Kent' is a frequent refrain in his journals. Or, 'We now pass from the Palace of 1690 built by Wren for William and Mary, to the additions constructed c. 1723 for George I by William Kent, and observe the great inferiority of the designs and decorations.' Some of these inferiorities were listed by George Vertue in his *Notebooks*, kept in the 1740s:

Niches of marble and pedestals with statues gilt with burnished gold which makes a terrible glaring show and truly Gothic, according to the weakness of the conception of the Surveyors and Controllers of the King's Works, or their private progress. . . . One ceiling which is a large long oval presents Jupiter coming to Danae, not in a Cloud of Gold, but of Snow. . . . Another is in Imitation of the Ancient Roman Subterranean Ornaments—poor Stuff. All these paintings are so far short of the like works done here in England before by Verrio, Cook, Streeter, Laguerne, Thornhill, Ricci, Pellegrini, etc., in Noblemen's Houses in Town and Country. . . .

As Queen Victoria at the beginning of her reign had given the Park to her people, so curiously enough one of her last acts was to have thrown open to the public her birthplace and first home where, early one morning, she had been summoned from her bed at six, put on a dressing-gown and seen Lord Conyngham fall upon his knees as he officially announced the King's death—while the Archbishop added details of a more personal nature. At nine, Lord Melbourne arrived in full court dress: 'It has long been my intention to retain your Lordship and the rest of the present Ministry at the head of affairs.' At half-past eleven, she held her first council.

Her bedroom and nursery, the cupola room in which she was baptized and the Presence Chamber in which that first council was held, can all be seen. For these rooms have become extensions, as it were, of the London Museum[1]—though long before this official designation the Palace had acquired from foreign royalty something of a reputation as a museum on account of its collection of pictures—Knellers, Gainsboroughs and Kauffmans. Yet it was not these that caught the eye of Peter the Great, since 'over the chimney in the royal sitting-room was a plate which, by an ingenious machinery, indicated the direction of the wind'; and with this plate, Macaulay adds, 'the Emperor was in raptures'. So it is today. The ingenious machinery is an iron rod that connects with a vane on the roof—and it still draws children with a scientific cast of thought, just as the blue singlet with the brown stains in which Charles I[2] was executed still draws the bloodthirsty. 'Yes, they would come just as readily to see me hanged.' Voltaire's cynicism is apt; he knew how on a day of public executions the town would

---

[1] Formerly, to be found up to 1941 in Lancaster House, off Green Park (see p. 105).
[2] See pp. 154-5.

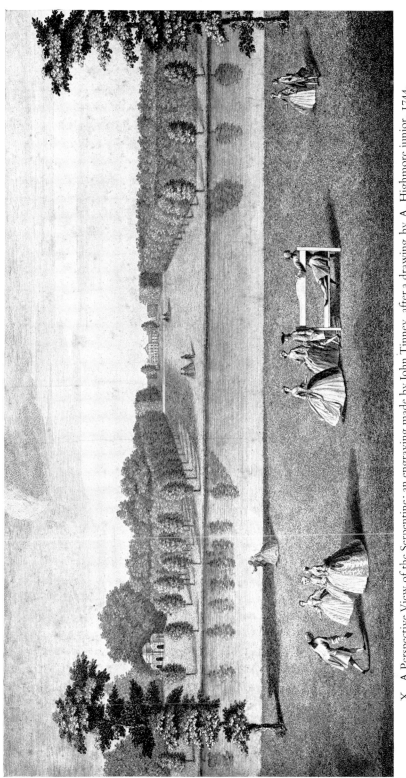

X. A Perspective View of the Serpentine; an engraving made by John Tinney, after a drawing by A. Highmore junior, 1744.

XI. 'On the Long Water'; an acquatint, one of a series of six, by Tristam Ellis, 1881.

turn the streets into a fair, the women flocking in their holiday dresses, just as they flocked to see King George II from a 'grand pavilion or tent under Kensington Garden wall' review Colonel Burgoyne's regiment of Light Horse. As soon as this display was over some 'pieces of a new construction, of a globular form, were set on fire, which occasioned such a smoke as to render all persons within a considerable distance entirely invisible, and thereby the better enabled in time of action to secure a retreat.'[1] Forty-eight hours later the King was dead. Had Voltaire been in Kensington then, the smoke in which all disappeared would doubtless have afforded him fine material to moralize on the transitory character of sovereignty, worldly pomp and human behaviour.

Above all, it is Queen Victoria's spirit that has left its greatest mark on these Gardens. From her nursery with her dumb-bells and dolls preserved in cases, the avenues and groves stretch out below. So many of the military heroes whom she honoured and decorated have been paraded in games along these paths. For a soldier's immortality is through death to a bronze statue on a granite block; and then back, by the thousand, to a tin or leaden replica—the delight of those who can re-enact his campaigns, marshal his troops and so win again the glory of a battle whose fate is as undecided as it was on the day when it was first fought.

Kensington Gardens in war-time had its own colours. Fond of pointing a moral, in a posthumous book of verses, Humbert Wolfe writes of children who organize races round the statue in memory of Rhodes, or the obelisk put up to Speke—the discoverer of the Nile, and as yet are too young to have any inkling that it is pioneers like these who

> die fighting to
> ensure the peace.

The Palace of which, as George V said 'no other stands so well', was allowed by his son, George VI, to be semi-commandeered by the military in 1940. There in the rooms surrounding the Jacobean quadrangle and under the clock tower, No. 34 Personnel Section had its Headquarters. On Friday soldiers would wait impatiently to be paid,

[1] *Read's Weekly Journal*, 25th October, 1760.

the click of their boots resounding down the marble hall. They would be formed up in Kensington Barracks, marched across the Drive of Palace Gardens, then ordered to duck as they passed under the hooped entrance to the Green (which marked Queen Victoria's height), and were a minute later called to a halt in the road leading to the Grace and Favour Apartments. For those who had so often charged as brigands, Red Indians or highlanders into the Park, the low-hooped entrance brought a new restriction as, whole columns breaking into file, would bring their rifles from the slope to the trail, while those at the back would sometimes make of the second's respite the pretended leisure to lean against their muzzles as though they were shooting sticks. 'Pick up the step . . .' 'Be late for the Judgment . . .' 'Get into line . . .' The scolding tones of Glasgow and Lancashire sergeants would harry Londoners unmindful as they passed York House of the site where once a wizened man used to crouch making chairs for dolls out of bone, upholstered in blue or red velvet, or of the old woman by the gate who used to sell badges for the boat-race, coconut ice and balloons the colour of muscat grapes. . . . For these war-time memories are like the dying footfalls of a column of men marching away, the memories of Hector and Lysander turning into the warm peaceful drone of bees, the sound that 'sumer is icumen in', that the cuckoo and rook are flying momentarily over the Gardens.

The *ailanthus altissima*, the tree of heaven, has always brought the bee to Kensington. The honey from a nearby apiary is described as having 'a delicious muscatel flavour'. As a girl Victoria wanted to find out all that she could about the lore of the honey-bee and later, when she married, she would listen to Prince Albert telling her how the sweetest honey came from the earliest flowers.

> A swarm of bees in May
> Is worth a load of hay . . .
> A swarm of bees in July
> Is not worth a fly.

As she continued with her cross-stitch, so she would think of all that he had learnt in 'beloved Rosenau'—the names of trees; deer-stalking; the mounting of butterflies. Was there any other prince in Europe who could rival his knowledge of botany, or who had mastered so much

XII. The Albert Memorial in the 1860's; a hand-coloured engraving by T. A. Prior, after a drawing by G. H. Andrews.

XIII. 'The New Ride'; a cartoon by John Leech, published in *Punch*, 1860.

Latin? In some of her churches there were stained-glass portraits of bishops holding hives—not a sign that they were patrons of bee-keepers or wax-refiners, but a symbol of their ambrosial eloquence in the pulpit.

Some of these windows were shattered in the *Blitzkreig*, and along the Flower Walk hands as yellow as candle-grease can be seen moving as they describe the incendiary bomb that destroyed one of Pugin's finest Lady chapels in Kensington, or the terrible direct hit that made dust of a famous Greek patriarch of the Fourth Century. These were moments when so easily there could have been a hardening of the heart, or a surrender to a hardening of the arteries. Meanwhile well-thumbed texts, once read by loved ones in the trenches under General Sir Redvers Buller, now again offered consolation to those widowed by past campaigns: 'Be not forgetful to entertain strangers for thereby some have entertained angels unawares.' Thus it was tucked away in small top rooms accustomed once to the scuttling feet of tweenies, these bereaved of Mons or Ladysmith waited for the knock that would summon them to live anew the victories and defeats of their dear ones made fresh by the news of Dunkirk, or the Sicily landings. Nor did this habit die with the war. All through the summer to the Flower Walk they come, leaning a little more heavily upon their sticks than they used to, and yet as careful as ever to leave before the park bell sounds.

The park bell sounds! What an antediluvian ring the words have, recalling the 'Seventies, 'Eighties and 'Nineties when a bell was used 'to muster people returning to town'. Then as soon as a party numerous enough to provide mutual protection had formed, they would begin the long hazardous journey through the Gardens and woodland to either the corner of Oxford Street or Piccadilly. In the reign of George III not a week passed without a robbery, and the park bell-ringers became as familiar a part of London life as the muffin-criers.

Today, half an hour before sundown, the rangers cry, 'All out of the Park, All out of the Park.' Their voices carry across the water into the lawless grass, their words blurring and growing indistinguishable from the sad baying of hounds. Sometimes the squabble of grebes as they fight for a covet breaks the monotony—or the bleating of a solitary sheep, until at last the Gardens are silent, the paths empty, the dells deserted, the gates padlocked. Over the sleeping moorland there is the stillness that once had brought the highwayman his purse, or the poacher his royal swan. Their witching hour as they used to lie in wait is now marked only by a sudden flight of starlings as they leave the branches between the Peter Pan statue and the Temple Lodge (on the left of Plate X, facing p. 42), rise sharply over the Serpentine, and in tremendous undulations slowly sink on extended wings into the darkness of Hyde Park.

KENSINGTON GARDENS.

SEASON TICKET—1850.

Allow *A. J. Stothard*

TO FISH IN THE SERPENTINE RIVER.

To Mr. Mann,
  10, Stafford Row, Pimlico.

Carlisle

A Season ticket for fishing on the Serpentine, 1850.

PART II

HYDE PARK

HYDE PARK

I

TO KNOW THE ropes is to rule Hyde Park. Ballad-mongers as well as Gaiety girls have sung and danced its changing fashions. Once it was the playhouse, the warm glow of candles in cockle-shells lighting the actors as the gallants in the boxes joined in and called for a

> gelding and rid to Hide Park
> On tantararara tantivee

as once, in the palmy days of Romano's, the audience had sung with Grace Palotta:

> Policemen smile
> As I go down the Park in style.

In 1823 fops would take a morning stroll from Cumberland Gate to Knightsbridge and then reappear between five and seven to repeat the performance. Because performance it was: 'They came to see, but also to be seen.' Fifteen years later it would have been considered vulgar to have promenaded before noon. For the Park has always had its social hours as well as seasons. Summer was definitely for the populace.

The great houses of Mayfair and Belgravia would be shut up, and on any August week-end soldiers would be seen parading in pairs, still wearing the plumed shakos of the Peninsula; they would be making for the bandstand to which others of their regiment would be marching from Victoria, led by a negro dressed in silks and a turban. Here was a living mascot of British success in the long fight against slavery. With a tambourine in one hand, this black major-domo would shake a rattle on a pole that would cause the servants left in town to pull back the shutters of the first floor and watch. Running along the narrow pavements would be children banging tins, their faces so pale that if they were cut they might be expected to bleed white: only the butcher boys, as they played their bones, glowed with a ruddy complexion. Then at Hyde Park Corner the noise would be swollen by the posthorn of the Kensington and Piccadilly coaches as the strains of a Rossini opera became lost in the general tumult of sound. Such was the street music of the 1840s caught by Cruikshank. In his sketches, the wealth and poverty of his mean and generous strokes point their own moral: the contrast between the rich embroidered trappings of the negro and the rattlebone features of the Savoyard by his hurdy-gurdy. In the days of the Welfare State, this is a London supposedly vanished—yet at this Corner when they open the gates a part of it still remains. . . .

'Steam tugs' is a way of asking for a bed without bugs. 'A twopenny hangover' is a rope suspended across a room, about a foot above a bench. Whereas Cockney rhyming slang has been made popular by the music-hall, tramp-slang remains practically unexplored. This is because there is no bounce in it—only a kind of protracted pain in the accuracy of its irony. For by the same counter as a night's rest over a rope is 'a twopenny' improvement on a seat on the Embankment, so the man who 'cuts' the rope at five sharp is called 'the valet'. Naturally there are degrees of down-and-out. Some have known better days; they can afford to say (as I remember hearing a Paddy say who had once been a stable boy in Wicklow), 'Sure, 'tis all a case of knowing the ropes.' Indeed, when such as he stumble upon half a crown in the grass, they can be certain of a night's lodging at a Rowton House together with a hot bath. But there are others who have not known better days; those who have been dispossessed from the beginning and to whom literally there is no further to go—save from the bench to the doss-house and from the doss-house back to the bench. These it is who rot first, growing unsexed as they become shunned by women (voluntary celibacy is quite another matter). In the end, physical or social ostracism prove more killing than either the sagging belly or the faulty lung. Again, it is these who know the shelters or orangeries of the parks as 'cough holes' and Notting Hill as 'Rotting Hill'. Combing the ground from east to west for cigarette butts, dropped change or the leavings from a picnic basket, occasionally a figure will break rank to share a crust with the sparrows. This may be the moment of return, the stopping of the rot. For it is a curious phenomenon of the parks how many of their tramps are bird-men.

'I have watched and become as a sparrow that sits upon the house-top.' From the high windows of Mayfair, on a clear morning it is possible to see the Serpentine. Before the day's traffic begins and the smell of petroleum mixes with the scent of limes, it is easy to make the journey back in time to the Domesday Book when the Manor of Hyde was part of the Estate of Eia. Easy to change the shapeless coat of the beggar into the smock of the serf. Now the sheep tracks that used to lead to the Manors of Neyte (Pimlico) and Eabury (Chelsea) have become congested—not the road for the cars as once it had been not the wood for the trees; but when there is a street diversion at Knights-bridge or Sloane Square with gangs working a few feet beneath the surface, it is simple to trace afresh the design of the city as it spreads over the land. The Great Fire of 1666 did not touch these parts because houses in profusion did not reach so far westwards—although three centuries later incendiaries were to expose beneath basement-level the charred remains of tree-trunks that had lain buried for over a thousand years. Thus it was, sometimes, that during the war old lags of the demolition squads proved themselves delinquent archaeologists.

In the Tenth Century, before these parts of the Estate of Eia could fall under the plough, they had to be cleared: the property had been bequeathed to the monks of Westminster by Geoffrey de Mandeville as a peace-offering in exchange for masses to be said for the repose of his soul, and within five centuries it was yielding an annual revenue of £14. Into the forests of Hyde, Neyte and Eabury they had cut fields, cultivating them in strict rotation. Against the Via Trinobantina (the present Bayswater Road), which was their northern boundary, a rich pattern of colours stretched as crops of corn turned to green in the forests of the sky-line; then sloping away to the south, the lighter hues of barley and wheat and yellow charlock would become shadowed in the purple of the clover. Some early park chroniclers refer to these higher fields as 'folds', to the lower as 'drips',[1] the latter being a term which may derive from the tendency of water to gather in low ground,

---

[1] Gerard Manley Hopkins uses these terms in his poetry, and there is plenty of evidence in his *Journals* to show that he had studied these early park chroniclers.

since it was in this low ground in the old Manor of Hyde in which Queen Caroline had the marshy pools joined and the Serpentine sunk.

Yet to the Benedictines at Westminster these ponds became more and more of a distraction. At the same time as St. Francis was preaching to the birds in Assisi, at home an anonymous writer had just issued a rule for anchoresses. He exhorted his brethren to remember the sparrow in the psalm of David that sat alone upon a house-top and imitate such an example. For thus it was that 'an anchoress should always offer the birdsong, as it were, of her prayers, alone and in a place of solitude.' Meanwhile, in the great Abbey church, the genuflexion of the monk grew more casual as he hurried from his chapter house to supervise those who tilled his land. He was pressed for time; there were royal guests to be attended to. In the woods, the hart, buck and doe waited to be hunted and, near the small stream of the Eye Burn (Tyburn), there were good coverts for water-fowl. And were water-fowl fish or meat—and if not meat, then could they be served on Fridays without danger to the laws of abstinence? There were abbots, other than Chaucer's, who also 'loved venerie', or

> To ryde on hawkinge by the ryver
> With grey goshawke in hande.

As these hunting parties passed, hay forks would be lowered and a man at his plough might shout of a boar's tusk or an ancient coin which he had found; but the news would be met with the same gesture that met the Thames fisherman as in return for a salmon the cellarer would reward him with bread and ale. The Church was growing prosperous; tithes were no longer offerings but expected gifts; the earlier spirituality was disappearing and in vain might religious be compared to

birds because they leave the earth, that is, the love of all worldly things, and because of the longing of their hearts towards heavenly things, fly upwards towards heaven; and although they fly high in a noble and holy life, they hold their heads low in gentle humility, just as a bird bows its head in flight; and they put no value on their own good works, saying that our Lord taught all His followers to say: *When you have done all things well, say, 'We are unprofitable servants.'*

London might still send its bands of pilgrims to Canterbury or Walsingham, led by a 'povre parsoun of a toun' whose love of his

XIVB. Male and Female Macaronies; a chapter-heading from Jacob Larwood's *Story of the London Parks*.

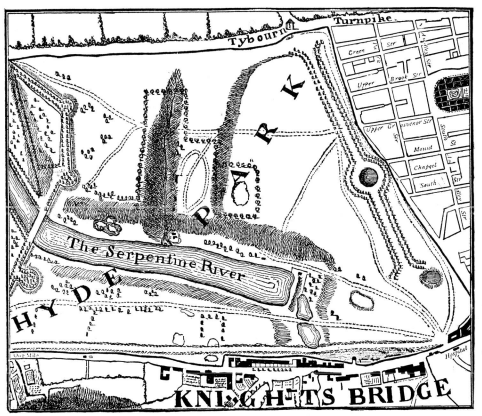

XIVA. A Map of Hyde Park in 1748 drawn by John Rocque.

XV. 'Outfall of the Serpentine at Knight's Bridge'; a painting 'from Nature and on Stone' by G. F. Philips, early Nineteenth Century

flock had preference to 'seken . . . a chaunterie for soules' at St. Paul's, but in the larger cathedrals and abbeys too often the sound of a slammed grill would reverberate beneath the soaring traceries. At last the time came 'when the light of the Gospel having dawned upon the King through the beautiful eyes of Anna Boleyn, that King drove the poor monks from their snuggeries and claimed the church lands'. Such at least is the verdict of Jacob Larwood in a chapter he wrote on Hyde Park in 1881; and if his style suggests a mixture between coyness and cosiness, it none the less represents an attitude of mind not so very far removed, except linguistically, from that of the Reverend John Langthorne who a century before had written in a letter: 'Good God! What outrages against reason, and thy pure religion, did it commit in the thirteenth century, when the extravagant Francis preached to swallows and fishes!'

How comes it then from spring to autumn that there now gather a group of speakers at Marble Arch whose circle includes hot-gospellers, Trade Union leaders, anarchists and racing tipsters as well as home-spun philosophers, Franciscans, Evangelists and rabbis? On Sundays and public holidays, have the views of Langthorne and Larwood became no more than the footnotes of dead history?

II

IT IS PERHAPS not so frivolous after all to begin working toward an answer by resurrecting a popular Gaiety chorus:

> If you would reign as a social queen
> You must always stick to the golden mean.

For the Park (and without a prefix that always means Hyde Park) has ever been famous for its social fashions. Within less than twenty years of it being given to Londoners by the Crown in 1637, dandies would be seen wearing spurs in order that the jingle set going might recall the rattling of Apollo's arrows mentioned in the first book of the *Iliad*. In 1796 Lady Caroline Campbell wore a feather four foot higher than her bonnet, and in the years that followed Waterloo there was much competition in dress between the sexes: waists there were none and as tier upon tier of furbelow and frippery were built up, so the men took to girding up their loins in order to make them as small as possible—'fine by degrees and beautifully less'. Such was the world of society, or of 'the upper ten thousand' as it came to be called. The Park was 'the show shop of the metropolis' said Pierce Egan—and the introduction of the word 'shop' is the key to what distinguishes the Park of Langford's or Larwood's day from that of Lansbury's, or our own day.

In the 'Nineties, shocking was still considered a fine art whose best parade ground remained the Park. Yet as early as July 1855 a number of shopkeepers had decided to hold an open-air meeting to protest against a Sunday Trading Bill. The Commissioner of Police, Sir Richard Mayne, forbade it. Three months later a carpenter took it upon himself to collect an audience and, encountering no hostility, he repeated the performance the next Sunday—congratulating his listeners on their good sense in meeting 'in their own park'. But in the next month there followed three riotous gatherings; on each occasion the police had to be called in to restore order. Then in 1859 a vast crowd assembled to present an address of sympathy to the Emperor Napoleon, assuring him of their admiration for the course which he had pursued in Italy, while in 1862 another vast crowd assembled to pledge their loyalty to Garibaldi—though this time the affair ended in some bloodshed.

Consequently when the Reform League approached Sir Richard about a mass rally in 1866, he refused permission. Yet undaunted they marched to the Park, where they found the police guarding the entrances (Plates XXX and XXXI, facing pp. 98 and 99). At this the reformers grew angry, pulled down the railings, and held their demonstration. Thus when the Commissioner of Police was next approached he arranged with the Commissioner of Works for a place to be assigned for meetings a hundred and fifty yards from 'the Reformer's tree', where the last riotous meeting had been staged. This is now universally known as Orators' Corner. So it was that as the fashionable world paraded up and down the East Carriage Drive, more and more would be drawn to Marble Arch to hear the latest political opinions; and, as the political opinions were questioned and argued and debated, so they soon led to religious opinions. At the turn of the century, Augustus Hare was able to observe: 'This spot has been used much . . . for Radical meetings, and on Sundays numerous open-air congregations on the turf . . . make the air resound with the "revival" melodies, and recall . . . Wesley and Whitefield.' The phrase 'on the turf' has an apt historic irony.

'I must be on horseback for life, if I would be healthy', noted Wesley in his journal, and at the time of the Great Exhibition when Henry Prince, 'the quondam Evangelical curate of Charlinch, was to be seen driving about Hyde Park', it was regularly 'in a carriage and four, preceded by hatless outriders', because they were 'in attendance upon the Lord'. Was this messianic megolomania, asked spectators—or was it just plain madness? 'In me you behold the love of God,' Prince would say—and who could quite fathom what strange spirits possessed a man who believed that he could not take up an umbrella without resort to prayer? Where are the dividing lines between coincidence and super-stition? Before the monks had taken over the Manor of Hyde, the property had belonged to the Anglo-Saxon Master of Horse; after them, it had been made into a racecourse at the Restoration and perhaps the jockeys had been none other than Satan's outriders? Or what of the story of a female charioteer who had driven her phaeton from Grosvenor Gate to Kensington in five and a half minutes— might not there have been invisible fiends whipping her bays on? Did he remember the history of James Nayler and the curious cavalcade which had met his return from the exterior darkness of prison when his followers seated him upon a mount, his hat well pulled over his eyes, while two women walking knee-deep through the muddy paths took the reins, while yet another man walked before him hatless, as those behind joined in with the ecstatic chant of 'Holy, Holy, Holy'?

Both Prince and Nayler were eccentrics—although unlike George Selwyn, who for forty years never missed an execution at Tyburn,[1] or Beau Brummel, who employed two shoe-makers, one for each foot—, they were eccentrics with this difference: namely, they were religious eccentrics. For if such men as Prince appear to be one in a thousand to their contemporaries, yet down the centuries their acts can be compared to those of at least a thousand other enthusiasts. Enthusiasm in politics or religion dies as hard as eccentricity in dress— and Hyde Park, sometimes separately, sometimes collectively, has always provided a propitious meeting-place for all three.

[1] The last occurred in 1783.

III

'TUESDAY WILL BE my good news-day . . .' 'May-day will be hey-day . . .' About these improvised catch-tunes—so infectious in a crowd—there is a suggestion of parties of six or seven, jostling and teasing each other, as their fairground hats invite the bolder to 'Cuddle Close' or 'Steal A Kiss'. These are the modern variations of bob-cherry or in-hurling. Only once did the Park ban its gates to them—and that was under the Puritans.

The Royalists had won several victories, and Parliament feared for the protection of London. On the First of May, 1643, digging began on the City's north-western frontier:

> ladies down to oyster-wenches
> Labour'd like pioneers in trenches.

Their aim was to build a large square fort with four bastions that might provide a stronghold for the righteous. Lady Eleanor went further; their act was foretold in Revelation and in a pamphlet printed at Knightsbridge she gave the cipher, but a cipher that showed as little respect for sense as syntax. 'And thou Hyde Park,' she begins,

> none of the greatest, yet makes up the harmony before the wedding all rejoicing. The trees of wood also utter their ayrie voice, where the court of guard's service is well worth the marking and observation; those bulwarks there so watcht round about; and here to proceed with the everlasting word of God, there the flaming sword also; the tree of life guarded thereby with turns every way on the east of it, and as it were the cherubim returned displaying in the air their golden wings, those colours of theirs. Like as the man when driven out to till the ground from whence he was taken, and so the thorn and the thistle and herb of the field his portion, with his wife sent away in their buff coats and skins to take their progress.

Some critics have dismissed this passage as a piece of Puritan fanaticism—and yet in its equating of Hyde Park with Paradise and the Roundheads with cherubim there is a kind of neutering process which may be only the reverse of the straight hair, the sad-coloured dress and the nasal whine so ready with quaint texts. For at this period stone-masons were employed to make decent nymphs and graces, and maypoles were hewn down; rope-dancing, bowls and horse-racing were forbidden—and a game of bob-cherry was considered to as ill become a reader of the Scriptures as romping beneath the mistletoe a believer in the birth of Christ. Under the Levellers, the Park became a mournful place, and in 1652 the Long Parliament sold it to private hands, every coach in future (as Evelyn noted) paying a toll 'of a shilling, and a horse sixpence, to the sordid fellow who had purchased it'.

Yet who can stop tendrils from putting forth new shoots, or the sap from rising? Puritanism warred with nature, and on the First of May, 1654, there was more a-Maying 'than for divers years past'. 'Much sin was committed by wicked meetings with fiddlers, drunkenness, ribaldry and the like', writes one newspaper. '. . . Came . . . many hundreds of coaches, and gallants in attire, but most shameful powder'd hair men, and painted and spotted women. . . . But his Highness the Lord Protector was not thither. . . .' It was a lie: he was there and so were many of his closest followers, for as another paper, *The Moderate Intelligencer*, comments when describing an in-hurling match: 'There was present his Highness the Lord Protector and many of the Privy Council.' Indeed, his appearance was the gossip of many letters dispatched that year.

In-hurling was a forerunner to rugby. A ball is tossed between two teams and their object is to place it in a goal three or four miles away (in out-hurling, say between Devon and Cornish men, the distance is increased and a parish church is chosen in each case as the goal). If tackled, a player may give up the ball, but it is 'both more generous and polite' to pass it to another, while he wrestles with his opponent. Consequently as many as eight or nine wrestling matches might occur in the course of a game. Sometimes the leather balls were cased in gold or silver, symbols of the sun that is also 'the Sunne of God', since in the Early Church the throwing of a ball up and down an aisle was a symbol of the sharing of the Son of God among a congregation. The day that Cromwell watched, 'the ball they played withal was silver, and designed for that party which did win the goal'.

If in retrospect there seems a kind 'of papist irony' in Puritans witnessing such a sport, then it was an irony which the lampoonists of the time were not slow to develop when two years later the Lord Protector's six greys, tasting his whip, took to plunging, plunged the postilion down, plunged his Highness down—his foot catching in the cross-bar, his head being dragged a quarter of a dusty mile, his pistol exploding in his pocket.

To satire, the Royalist broadsheets added prophecy:

> Every day and hour has shown the power,
> And now he has shown us his art.
> His first reproach was a fall from a coach
> And his next will be from a cart.

But the unknown versifier was something of a plagiarist and underrated his opponent. 'Your Highness may see by this that you have the voice of the people as well as God,' said a flatterer of the cheering crowd that had been assembled to meet the Protector on his return from Ireland. 'As to God,' he answered, 'we will not talk about Him here; but for the people they should be just as noisy if they were going to see me hanged.' Then he turned to inspect his troops, with their sea-green ribbons in their hats. Had a man of ninety been in that crowd to hear the tumult of salutation as Colonel Backstead's regiment fired a volley, he might have recalled how as a boy he had been brought to the same field to see Queen Elizabeth muster her pensioners, arrayed in the green and white cloth of the Tudor colours.

Unlike Kensington Gardens (except in the last fifty years), the Park has often served as an open-air barracks. Pikemen, musketeers and dragooners have all pitched camp beneath its trees. Sometimes the military have been the toast of the town, sometimes the joke, and sometimes they have been heartily detested. Their popularity, it has been said, has fluctuated as much as the length of a gown: in a sense it might be nearer the truth to say that the world of fashion and military dress have both interacted upon each other.

Horsemanship and whoresmanship have points in common. The pun is Shakespearian in origin—though only once have I seen it played up in a production of *Henry V*.[1] Certainly 'the Ring' was a scene to both (Plate XIVA, facing p. 52).

'The Ring', which used to lie just north of the Serpentine (not far from the present boat-houses), is described best by a Sixteenth Century traveller from France. It is 'two or three hundred paces in diameter, with a sorry kind of balustrade, or rather with poles placed upon stakes, but three feet from the ground, and coaches drive round this. When they have turned for some times round one way, they face about and turn t'other. So rolls the world.' Here the magnificence displayed on the First of May, 1660, drew forth from Evelyn the sentiment: 'It was the Lord's doing. Such a restoration', he continued, 'was never mentioned in any history since the return of the Jews from the Babylonish captivity.' Old Cavaliers drank their Sovereign's health as many times as they could still rise to their feet, Edgehill was freshly remembered in their cups, and they peppered every speech with a 'damn', 'blast' or 'a pox' that two years before would have earned them a fine.

Meantime, Pepys aboard the *Naseby* watched the Royal Standard flying from Deal Castle. Above were fine-weather bales of clouds—promising auguries, though unlike the captain of the ship he did not bother to count them. His heart instead was heavy since he was sad not to be able to wave to his friends in 'the Ring', and that night he ended the entry in his diary thus: 'it being a very pleasant day, I wished myself in Hyde Park.'

Three years later his wish came true. He was able to go a-Maying—only to be sadly disappointed: 'Here I saw nothing good—neither the King, nor my Lady Castlemaine nor any great ladies or beauties being there, there being a great deal more pleasure on an ordinary day; or else those good faces that there were being choked up with many bad ones, there being people of all sorts in coaches there to some thousands.' The sole admiration he could raise was for 'the King's riders showing tricks'.

Such displays became as regular a feature as the foot races round 'the Ring' had been. For the opening of the Park, James Shirley had written

[1] At the Old Vic during a season in which Paul Rogers played the part of the Dauphin (1949).

XVI. The Cake House, Hyde Park, late Eighteenth Century; a water-colour by Thomas Hearne.

XVII. The Cake House, Hyde Park, 1823; a wash-drawing by J. T. Serres.

a play in which, before the jockeys appear, an English and Irish foot-man begin the racing. The piece, which is set in the Park, abounds with allusions to the singing of birds, notably the cuckoo and nightingale, while, in the interval between the foot- and horse-race, a milkmaid goes round crying out 'milk of a red cow'—a current antidote for musty superfluity. The drama—'a very moderate one', according to Pepys—was revived in 1668, a time when it was rapidly becoming the habit to visit the Park after the playhouse; and as the manners of the promenaders and riders were imitated by actors and the ways of soldiers held up to both ridicule and admiration, so in turn this led to a rivalry in which commanders of their troops grew anxious also to show off what their men could do. Naturally in such reviews horsemanship was a large part of the spectacle. At the last one which Charles II attended, after the Guards had shown off their jumping, their wheeling in formation and a musical 'ride', their guests replied by galloping at full speed, their lances ready to hook rings from the ground which as soon as they had spiked they then proceeded to juggle. This feat, still common in Morocco, was known as *fantasias*.

So it was that as 'the Ring' became more and more discussed on the stage, its merits became a point of debate. Says Lady Malapert in a comedy by Southerne, 'There are a thousand innocent diversions more wholesome and diverting than always the dusty mill-horse driving in Hyde Park.' 'O lor', retorts her husband, 'don't profane Hyde Park. Is there anything so pleasant as to go there alone and find fault with the company? Why, there can't a horse or a livery 'scape a man that has a mind to be witty; and then, I [chaff] the orange-women.' Even early in the reign of Charles II, the Mall in St. James's was growing into a serious rival. Says a young lady of quality in a piece by Etherege: 'I abominate the dull diversion of "the Ring", the formal bows, the affected smiles, the silly words and amorous tweers in passing. [In the Mall] one meets with a little conversation now and then.'

By the reign of Queen Anne, trick riding and novelties such as syllabub, pigeon-pie puff and cheese-cake had become so essential a part of watching the entertainments that one satirist, recalling the Moorish *fantasias* and 'other fantasticks', called the Park, 'The Circus, or British Olympus', while Price's Refreshment Lodge of the previous century became renamed the Cake House, or Mince Pie House[1] (Plates XVI and XVII, facing pp. 60 and 61). Mrs. de la Riviere Manley, a native of Guernsey, taking her cue from the anonymous author of 'The Circus' wrote a satire about the London 'Prado', which was so incestuous in implication ('So rolls the world') that it was lodged in the Queen's Bench on a charge of *scandalum magnatum*. Yet the greater the libel the greater the truth . . . and so the case was never heard.

'Neither frost, nor snow nor an east wind', declared the *Spectator* writers, 'hinders people from going [to "the Ring"].' 'Neither dust nor heat in June', added the *Tatler* writers. In fact so intense was the rising heat that a German traveller, in a letter home in 1716, speaks of a man being sent with a barrel to sprinkle the ground in preparation for the day's traffic. The dust, however, was fashion's friend; seldom could the same dress be worn twice and there were ever Malaperts to find fault. 'Bless me, sir! What strange, filthy fellow was that you bow'd to . . . ?'

In high seclusion, Larwood could let the dados creep up his Victorian study walls, his mahogany desk be exchanged for one of Annish days, while in his manuscript of *The Story of the London Parks* he could compare 'the Ring' to Hell. He had in mind not Mrs. Manley's account of the 'Prado', but rather Cardinal Bellarmine's description of the bottomless pit as a place particularly terrible for its heat and over-crowding. To belong to the unwashed was the worst crime—and how far his England had advanced since the Eighteenth Century! As the tea grew cold in the willow pattern, he let slip unemphasized the tale of a handkerchief thief caught by the 1771 crowd and handed to a soldier to be ducked in the Serpentine, an extra dousing to be administered for each handkerchief on the principle that 'this wets me more than it does you'. Only rather vaguely did the author assume that a ducking for 'delinquents of that kind . . . was supposed [also] to wash them clean of their sins'. Why, at the very moment that he was writing, was there not talk of making the existence of God a party issue? Larwood continued with his fund of anecdotes and facts—though to follow him thus is to anticipate history. . . .

[1] Today there exists the Ring Tea House (1908) where light luncheons and snacks are served in the summer, and in Kensington Gardens there is a Refreshment Pavilion on the road leading to the Alexandra Gate.

For 'the Ring' began to fall out of fashion in the 1730s, while on the 6th December, 1736, *The London Spy* announced: 'The Ring . . . being quite disused by the quality and gentry, we hear that the ground will be taken in for enlarging the Kensington Gardens.' Queen Caroline had plans for a serpentine lake as the King too had plans for a new carriage road, a *route du roi*—or the Rotten Row of the future. Yet she was even more ambitious than her sovereign lord. Let His Majesty's engineers hasten to begin work on this new drive, but let Mr. Charles Withers hasten to her. There would be waters playing in emulation of Versailles and there would be yacht-racing through the summer. While the King thought of his latest carriage, his steeds straining upon their bits, her mind swirled with the promise of sea-horses. The Doge of Genoa had once sent her squirrels. Perhaps now he might send her a fleet of dolphins.

IV

'ONE MAN MAY lead a horse to water, but twenty cannot make him drink,' said Dr. Johnson, shying away with a nice sense of independence from the proverbial cliché. Running neck and neck, as it were, the Serpentine and Rotten Row have frequently invited competition as well as comparison between their aquatic and equestrian displays.

This rivalry dates back to the reign of George II, since if the Queen's lake showed only one bend in spite of its intended snaking course, then the King's mile and a half of row ran a straight but bumpy course. So far there has been mentioned one possible derivation of its name from *route du roi*; others have claimed a Celtic derivation, arguing that the name comes from *rattanreigh*, which means a good mountain path as opposed to a bad one. John Timbs in his believe-it-or-not miscellany of the 1870s, *Thing Not Generally Known*, suggests that the name can be traced to *rotteran*, to muster—'a military origin which may refer to the Civil War'. Like much else in Timbs' book of curiosities, this is rather far-fetched since the Row appears for the first time in Eighteenth Century maps and its first mention occurs in 1737 in the *London Spy Revived*: 'The King's Road . . . is almost gravelled and finished, and lamp-posts are fixed up. It will soon be levelled and the old road [i.e. the present South Carriage Drive] levelled with the Park.' Yet the new Row was so convex that it made the old road seem concave: 'Both agree in the common of being . . . impassable,' declared Lord Hervey at the end of 1737.

Two years after its supposed completion the Duke of Grafton's carriage was upset 'in a deep pit' and the Duke's collar bone was dislocated—an accident that followed fast on a crash of the King's four daughters in a chaise at the same spot. Quickly the Princesses had been carried to Kensington Palace where their gentlewomen made ready to bathe their hurts with Eau de Carme, Hungary Water and Eau de

XVIII. A Review of the London Volunteer Cavalry and Flying Artillery in Hyde Park, May 1804; a coloured print issued a year later by John Wallis.

XIX. 'Preparing for a Mock Trafalgar on the Serpentine'; a print of 1814.

Luce. Yet deep ruts and darkness were small dangers beside those of highway robbery, or the stray gun-shot of an over excited duellist. In short, not until the pot-holes had been filled, the boulders dug up and the mud-flats been drained, did the unevenness of the Row acquire a legendary character; but by then, towards the close of the century, a new surface of fine gravel mixed with tan had been laid along this stretch of mile to soften the fall of both novice and dare-devil. The title 'Rotten' had become so much an anachronism that the *Public Advertiser* in seeking 'the friendly aid' of the Head Ranger could afford to pun in asking him to prevent 'the once admired lawn next the Serpentine from now very properly being called *Rotten* Row' on account of the dust caused by those riders who insisted on making their way to the water's edge.

When Mr. King spoke the prologue to the first performance of Sheridan's *Pizarro*, he could anticipate a cheer from the gallery at the lines:

> Horsed in Cheapside, scarce yet the gayer spark
> Achieves the Sunday triumph of the Park;
> Scarce yet you see him, dreading to be late,
> Scour the New Road, and dash through Grosvenor Gate:
> Anxious—yet timorous too—his steed to show,
> The hack Bucephalus of Rotten Row.

But the cheer did not echo all through the house. There were those to whom it was an affront and to whom a hiss in the darkness of the auditorium was safer than a challenge to meet at dawn, or the risk of being pelted by eggs. These 'travelled young men' were known as the Exquisites—primarily because of their tastes in dress and manners. For their Continental taste in food, at their own Savoir Vivre Club in St. James's Street, they were later christened the Macaronies.[1]

Pepys and his friends had sometimes spoken of 'the Ring' as 'the Tour'; now the idea of the Grand Tour came to take the place of 'the Ring'. At home, only slowly did the Row become a circus of display, or a hub of fashion, because the Macaronies were constantly changing

---

[1] In the season of 1770 Sir Joshua Reynolds saw Lady Melbourne with the Duchess of Ancaster and Lady Fordyce all dressed like men at a masquerade, 'the pretty fellows appearing in Dominoes as masculine as many of the macaroni things we see everywhere'. Compare this with Pepys's observations—see p. 97.

their habits. When they had been called the Exquisites they had been compared to gipsies in their love of a new pitch—though, reading between the lines, by pitch their critics may have meant vocal as well. For in peacetime, during the Eighteenth Century, a soldier's life provided a good opportunity for dressing up—and such was the main preoccupation of the Exquisite or Macaroni.

If a mosquito-net in Mark Antony's camp drove Horace to protest, how much more his imitators found to scorn in those quartered in the Park under the first three Georges. In straining the liquid to get rid of a mosquito, the peeping journalists of Grub Street often discovered that they had swallowed a swarm. In the end, their parodies of the Latin poet led to them satirizing themselves. . . .

'Look at the gay tents . . .' and within a dozen lines they have made them 'gay pavilions'. Draw aside the tent flaps and beneath the finest Brussels lace slumbers a gentleman a-bed, his wig powdered for the morrow, his boots blackened *au vin de champagne*. Pull aside the inner curtains and there sleeps his man—a rough fellow but one who will serve to make a dish of tea and keep a cellar (a portable cellar was part of the baggage of an Exquisite in the field). . . . Here was the material for another ode. It was only a thousand pities that a guard had been posted to prevent such a versifier from seeing the black Lacedemonian broth, 'i'sooth, I mean coffee,' as it was drained from a silver chalice that had been looted by 'rubinose Noll' a century ago; but the guard had stood firm and imagination must perforce supplement what the eye could not see in his noble H——s' pavilion. Again, as he protected his victim with an initial, so would he protect his own verse with the initial of his surname.

The next day strolling before noon and already castigating 'the ladies for wearing red cloaks like soldiers,' 'a Cato Censorius' would be preparing to pinion an Exquisite with his quill. The quill and the quiver, a happy conceit—and away would shoot the arrows to point out the gilt gorget, the dangling cane from the third regimental button, the rattle of dice and the snuff box opened with as much desire to flaunt a diamond ring as Venus rising from the waves. Then into the note-book would slip a certain self-righteousness, tempered with the more open insult—both protected by the *nom de plume*. Why was not this

66

effeminate monkey planning how to defeat Vauban, or Corhorn, or the American slave traders? Later, when the Exquisite became known as the Macaroni, under the same *nom de plume* another scribbler would admit how 'some of the tribe' did occasionally leap a ditch to encourage their men to bridge a marsh, but would deplore the '*plain* clothes' to which they returned after their military duties. The italics tell their own tale. Plain clothes could mean a white frock coat, every seam trimmed in golden cording, with cuffs of blue satin and a waistcoat to match. Indeed, one Macaroni captain not caring for the unmannerly way of ordering troops to 'Fire', used to post himself at the flank of his battalion, pull out a lace cambric handkerchief perfumed with ambergris and, with his nostrils held lightly between forefinger and thumb, scream: 'You may shoot now, soldiers.' 'Look down!...' cried many voices from Grub Street. 'Look down, immortal Granby, and blush for degeneracy of British commanders....'

These were of course the exceptions, the colourful eccentrics that inevitably send a report after them; and, without them, how dull would be many a news sheet printed under the Hanoverians! Yet not in all ways were these military eccentrics as effeminate as they are sometimes made out. By the reign of George III, the designs on their snuff-boxes were growing bolder; Venus had risen a thousand times from the waves—and surely there were other beauties—Lady Archer, for instance, whose face as it aged began to copy in enamel what the artist had made immortal twenty years ago, or Mrs. Hodges who could fly over a five-barred gate with as much speed as into a lover's arms. 'It was remarked that she had all the properties of Dian—except her chastity', said *The Times*. Snuff-boxes can provide their own commentary, even if it is a little less direct in manner than *The Times* or the columns and odes of the peeping journalists. For behind the beauties of the day, which they preserve, stretch away watery wastes—though it were better to call them watery graveyards, because if the secret will out they were often the pools for drowning illegitimate children. Among them, a frequent resort for both the Exquisite and Macaroni, were the eleven pools which Charles Withers had made into the Serpentine.

Withers had employed two hundred men in damming up the

Westbourne, and then digging channels beneath the pools. When this had been done, the dyke was opened and within a few days two yachts had been launched 'for the diversion of the royal family'. On the north-western shore, a mound had been made of surplus earth, crowned by a summer-house in the form of a Temple (this can be seen in A. B. Lens' wash-drawing of 1736—Plate VII, facing p. 37). Naturally the classical illusion was intended as a consistent part of the landscape gardening of the period. Only now in retrospect does the Temple appear a symbol of the overlapping severity and frailty of the age; for as the summer-house was set upon a pivot and subject to the winds, so too were the severe lines of the frail gowns that repeatedly passed in and out of fashion. The Exquisite, and later the Macaroni, had never lacked for feminine rivals—even if it were to be some years before 'the gentler sex could find a promenade' in which to meet them on their own ground. That first opportunity came in 1776 (Plate XIVB, facing p. 52).

The winter had been hard and the Serpentine had frozen over.[1] Throughout the countryside wagons had been 'frostbound like ships in Arctic seas.' The Row was deserted and for a brief few weeks the ice became an arena for displays of daring. £50 was offered to the first man to skate a mile in less than a minute; fifty guineas had been won by an Irish footman who was said to have skated eight miles in ten minutes.

The last year of the century witnessed a similar 'Great Frost'. Those who had been young thirty years ago taunted the new generation with the daring of their previous feats—many of them imaginary—, so that the new generation, determined not to be outshone, resorted to

---

[1] The same was true in 1826, when 'the most daring feat of all times was carried out on the Serpentine'. This was known as 'Extraordinary Exploit, or Crossing the Serpentine' (Plate XX, facing p. 68). Beneath the original lithograph there appears this description: 'On Tuesday, the 17th January, 1826, Mr. Henry Hunt for a bet of 100 guineas made with a Noble Lord of Sporting Celebrity drove his Father's Matchless Blacking Van with four blood horses upon the ice of the Serpentine at the broadest part:—he accomplished the hazardous task in the grandest style without the smallest accident.—The Picture represents his return to the North Bank from which he had set out amid the acclamations of the multitude.' The incident was pictorially presented by many different London papers the next morning, but the lithograph by Ingrey & Madeley remains by far and away the best. Copies of it were sold in the Strand at the time.

XX. 'Extraordinary Exploit, or Crossing the Serpentine'; a lithograph sold and made by Ingrey & Madeley after the event, 1826.

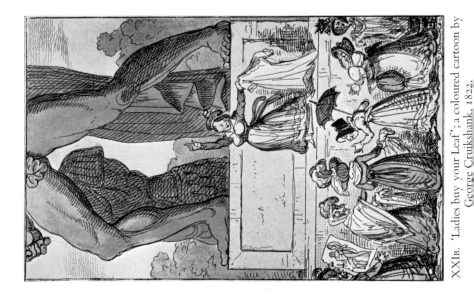

XXIB. 'Ladies buy your Leaf'; a coloured cartoon by George Cruikshank, 1822.

XXIA. 'The Wellington Statue'; a black and white cartoon by John Leech, 1846.

their own kinds of daring. Pink, coquilot and scarlet became the colours of the day, while their costumes, copied from Republican France, were based on Greek and Roman models. Then as the taunting grew stronger, so the craze for dress turned to one of undress. Biblical texts were juxtaposed with legends: 'Make way for this Lady Godiva who is naked and not ashamed!' The scribblers were quick to circulate their halfpenny broadsheets and the crowd determined not to be out-done, would extemporize with their own versions of popular songs. The couplet from 'The Banks of Banna',

> Shepherds, I have lost my love,
> Have you seen my Anna?

became:

> Shepherds, I have lost my waist,
> Have you seen my body?

'Bare shoulders' was a feminine rule adhered to with all the strictness of a military order.

When the last summer of the century arrived, the winter line dropped another inch, petticoats were shortened and for the first time muslin and tulle were introduced. The new fashion was called *ventum textile*, or woven wind—and the classical illusion from Petronius was intended. After all, it was argued, was there not poetry as well as poetic irony in imitating those Roman beauties whose lords had once conquered *Londinium*? It was a brave Macaroni who retaliated that if poetry repeated itself as much as the poets each other, then surely had not Mayfair sprung from the forest-home of the painted savage and anyhow, pray, what was the difference between woad and drops of hartshorn? From a periodical published in 1799, here is an extract taken from a conversation between a lady and her milliner:

'I am just come to town, Mrs. Furbelow, so have the goodness to inform me how I must appear to be in fashion.'

'That can be done in a moment, my lady; in two minutes I shall equip you in the first of the style: have the goodness to take off the bonnet.'

'Very well.'

'Please to take off that gown.'

'There it is.'

'Away with those petticoats.'

'There they go.'

'Throw off that handkerchief from your shoulders.'
' 'Tis done.'
'Away with those stays and sleeves.'
'Will that do?'
'Yes, my lady, now you are quite in the fashion. You see it is an easy matter. To be dressed in the fashion you have only to undress.'

Within a few months, the Eighteenth Century was over. There was a general feeling that life would never be quite the same. Already, it was rumoured, the satirists and cartoonists had shown a dreadful decline in the last decade. History would not repeat itself—only the historians. Yet, 'we shall see, we shall see,' continued to mumble a bearded figure under a narrow-brimmed hat as he ambled his white palfrey down the Row. Some said that he was contemplating the vanity of the new age; others said that they imagined things—and perhaps not without reason, since it was this rider's habit to paint his steed with black spots and streaks of purple. Caricatures began to appear at the same time as advertisements for hairs 'from the venerable beard of Hippocrates' at a guinea each. 'Of use to the fair that want fine children', ran the posters in Mount Street. 'I can tell them how; it is a secret. . . .'

Martin van Burchell had lived to carry eccentricity from one century to the next. For it was not the vanity of the age he pondered—nor the success of the revolutionary armies under Napoleon. His discourse was with the ranks of cherubim on the finer points of metaphysical argument; but one day, when his thoughts were less high flown, there came to him the notion of elastic bands and pulleys and the distribution of weight. He became the inventor of braces. And what gentleman and officer a-bed that morning would say that the invention had not been heaven sent to the new age?

V

THE DATES 1066 and 1815 act like dividing lines in English history. For as the Norman Conquest separates the Anglo-Saxon and mediaeval world, so the Battle of Waterloo separates an unmechanized world from a mechanized one. Whereas Dr. Johnson in his novel, *Rasselas*, could imagine the possibility of aerial invasions so, at the end of the Nineteenth Century, H. G. Wells could write with much more certainty of them; in-between, balloon ascents had become an accepted fact. Again, as the Age of Reason became the Age of Industrial Revolution, so the gaming tables counted for less; the sums hazarded at faro grew progressively smaller; high-scale gambling was transferred to the Stock Exchange. The Bartolozzi stags[1] on the Albert Gate lent the name of 'stags' to railway shares, because of the nearness of this Park gate to Hudson House, the home of the Railway King. Duelling became extinct, the last recorded fight in the cockpit being that between a Captain Macnamarra and a Colonel Montgomery in 1803,[2] while in its place was introduced boxing—thanks largely to the patronage of the Prince of Wales and the Dukes of Hamilton and Queensberry. Tom Cribb, Dutch Sam and the Game Chicken—all heroes of 'the new ring'—gave a fierce account of their fists to the public. Again, if the two avenues of walnut trees that flanked the West Carriage Drive had sometimes appeared singularly ominous after a long day's training to those preparing to defeat Napoleon, on their return home they were garlanded with festoons and illuminated at night with Chinese lanterns. The peace festivities held to welcome the veterans of Nelson and Wellington were on a scale that have never subsequently been surpassed in size or splendour.

Hyde Park became one seething fairground. Brewers' drays, laden

[1] More of their history is given in the chapter on 'Green Park' (see p. 127).
[2] Edmund Blunden has written a long, fine narrative poem about this duel called, 'Incident in Hyde Park, 1803'.

with hogsheads of draught porter, made their way from stall to stall. Booths advertised 'the fattest ladies of forty in the world'; monkeys danced with dwarfs dressed as Harlequins, and Columbines with dogs dressed as Cossacks. In marquees, sword-swallowers and fire-eaters were used as decoys for selling trinkets, hot mutton pies, and sand from the plains of France. Nets stretched between trees offered leafy bivouacs for feeding, with military music attending good appetite. A hand-press was set up to issue a programme of Park glories past and future, every copy being stamped with prints of 'War Heroes' whose popularity a few days earlier in the Row had caused them to declare the friendliness of the London multitude more terrifying than any hostile cavalry that they had met in the field.

July 31st was to be the grand gala night. As darkness fell, Trafalgar was to be re-enacted on the Serpentine (Plate XIX, facing p. 65). Fourteen British sail-of-the-line had been made of canvas, painted with guns and portholes, and mounted on small rowing boats. When the sun had set, the foremost ship-of-the-line got under way and opened fire upon the French. The battle began at eight—and by ten to nine it was over. The spectators began to troop towards St. James's and Green Parks for the promised firework display. But the crush was so tremendous that few could move; those that were forced to stay were well rewarded. For suddenly an English man-o'-war was seen ablaze, and there fell a dreadful hush over the crowd; then equally suddenly the hush rose into a triumphant shout as it was realized that she was bearing down upon the remaining French fleet. The enemy squadron sank amid jeers, cat-calls and the National Anthem.

Nothing so spectacular had ever been seen—even the tableaux at the Vauxhall Pleasure Gardens paled by comparison. Yet the fair, like any Pleasure Gardens, drew its full quota of mountebanks, confidence tricksters and thieves. The pick-pockets, as they skimmed dangerously along the water's edge, worked happily in the philosophy that those born to hang do not drown. The revelry inevitably led to debauchery and the Protestant Bishops protested. A woman stripped herself naked, preparing to bathe amidst the encouraging shouts of the men—but was rushed from the scene by a group of ladies dressed in black. The fair had cost the Government over £40,000, and a speaker in the House rose to remonstrate about the incredible scenes of vice it had encouraged and to register 'the infinite annoyance it had caused all the middle classes of society'. If the festivities had been held to honour Nelson and Wellington, then a woman had not only shamed her sex but the Serpentine's tribute to Trafalgar. Amends would be made—decided the Countess of Spencer; amends in the name of the Ladies of Britain. To the hero of the Battle of Waterloo, restitution as well as proper recognition should be paid.

Yet such was no more than the language of diplomacy. Put more truly, for some time the Countess and a few friends with artistic yearnings had longed to erect a monument that in part should be a copy of the Dioscuri on the Monte Carvallo, Rome. The Duke's name was simply an excuse for issuing a subscription list to swell the funds and so speed the project. No one save the Spencer Committee quite knew what the work was to be, because although a letter was sent out announcing that the figure 'would be a facsimile of a statue of Phidias, representing Alexander the Great taming Bucephalus', none of the ladies in Britain seemed to question the fact that Phidias had died almost a century before Alexander. Nor did the King, who allotted fifty feet of Park land for the granite base; nor the Pope, when he generously lent the casts; nor the Ordnance Office, which allowed twelve 24-pounders captured from the French to be melted down.

In 1822, therefore, an undraped Achilles was unveiled, which was really an adaptation of one of the horse-tamers from the Monte Carvallo in Rome. But who was to say where to lay the blame? As a sop to the conscience of the subscribers, Westmacott had placed the head of the Duke on the Homeric body. The figure had cost over £10,000, and its size and weight (thirty-three tons) made it such that it could not pass through any gate of the Park. Instead, part of the wall had to be knocked down, a reminder of the breach that used to be made in a city's defences when Olympian victors were carried home in triumph.

There was an immediate outcry. Cartoonists such as Cruikshank rushed for their drawing-boards (Plate XXIb, facing p. 69),[1] whilst

---

[1] It is interesting to contrast Cruikshank's reaction to the Achilles statue with that of Leech to the Wellington statue (Plate XXIa, facing p. 69) in 1846.

Sheriff Perkins in the columns of the *Morning Herald* told readers that if his mother, who was a Godfearing Newcastle woman, 'had caught any of her children looking at such an object, she would have soundly whipped them'. Another declared that, 'Westmacott ought to devote himself wholly to the representation of nymphs'. Leigh Hunt thought that, 'the figure seemed to be manifesting the most furious intentions of self-defence against the hero whose abode it was looking at'. Thus the West Carriage Drive, which had recently grown to be known as Wellington Drive, became deserted, and the Row, having suffered a decade's eclipse, now returned to fashion.

Meanwhile from Apsley House faithful retainers would look out on the changing scene. In his study, with its plain bedstead and table of books, their master was more than probably preparing a speech, deciding where to place the accents. Was it *Placetne vobis, Doctores; placetne vobis, Magistri,* or *Placetne vobis, Doctŏres; placetne vobis, Magistri.*[1] A false quantity could prove as untrue as an underfed soldier. . . . Then a shout would echo across the hall. A servant would be snatched from a telescope as he peered past the bullet-proof shutters trying to make out the inscription that seemed to set even language at defiance:

TO ARTHUR DUKE OF WELLINGTON
AND HIS BRAVE COMPANIONS IN ARMS
THIS STATUE OF ACHILLES
CAST FROM CANNON TAKEN IN THE VICTORIES
OF SALAMANCA, VITTORIA, TOULOUSE AND WATERLOO
IS INSCRIBED
BY THEIR COUNTRYWOMEN

There would follow another shout, sharper in tone. This was the Iron Duke under whom he had served—the living hero whose last crowning battle within twenty-five years was to lend its name to seven bridges in Europe; nine museums; seventeen public squares; and more than twenty streets. The spirit of the peace-festivities had died. If the making of a breach for the statue of Achilles had seemed for some a symbol of triumphal entry for the hero whom they venerated, then only two years had to elapse before an extension of the grounds of Apsley House

[1] He plumped for the latter on the day, apologizing after: 'Mr. Chancellor, which is it?'

74

was met with a public statement that 'if his sovereign gave him all Ireland for his estate, he would beg the Isle of Man for a cabbage garden'. Windows were broken as the mob grew angry. But the Duke remained unmoved. He had always believed popularity to be the quest of the idle man.

In the 1830s again, he was to suffer the venom of the mob as a result of the Reform Bill; in the 'Forties, he was to hear the M.P. for Finsbury shouted down for suggesting a second Hyde Park Fair. Then, as the 'Fifties approached, talk turned to commandeering a site for the World's Fair, or Great Exhibition. Secluded in his private garden, the Duke's thoughts also turned to one, Anne Hicks. At the east end of the Serpentine, near a spring well, she had kept an apple-stall (Plate XXIV, facing p. 80); later against the rain, she had stretched a tarpaulin and, against the wind, she had driven a semicircle of stakes about her. In a few years what had been little more than a temporary shelter had become a cottage. One day the order to quit had been issued. She had refused and was finally evicted—though not without much protest by her fellow supporters against this 'infraction of the rights of a private person by the Government'. There was one law for the rich and one for the poor. The Duke looked at his own garden with its limes! What a furor its acquisition had brought upon his head. He remembered how he had always chosen his aides-de-camp and favourite generals from men of family and high connections. His victorious army, he had said, were 'the scum of the earth, enlisted for drink'. He was diehard—and not afraid to admit it. When the crowd cheered, he was indifferent, or pointed a finger at the walled windows or shutters which they had forced him to put up to protect his property. Anne Hicks was safely tucked away in an almshouse; but was the huge glass archipelago of which Paxton had produced plans so wise after all?

VI

AFTER OPENING THE Liverpool Albert Dock, such had been the heat and excitement of the day, that the Prince Consort wrote: 'I am satisfied that if the population . . . had been weighed this morning, and were to be weighed again now, they would be found many degrees lighter.' Such simple scientific deductions were a recurring factor in his letters; they were a form of mid-century arithmetic in keeping with a desire for massed bands or marches from 'Athalie'. For the Victorian age was in full swing and society was particularly willing to be martialled by the conductor's baton. Solidity in numbers went with solidity in song. The World's Fair, which began as a monument to the industry of all nations, was within six months to be both transplanted and transformed into a musical conservatoire just outside of London.

From the beginning, Sir Robert Peel had supported a motion for a site in the Park. The first opposition came in *The Times*: a suburb would be more suitable—perhaps Sydenham, suggested one reader. The motion, however, was carried—though no sooner had the sappers finished their work and the glass edifice begun to rise than opposition came from other quarters, notably the Nonconformists and the Protestants. Whereas the latter proclaimed that it would be used as a rallying-point by the riff-raff of any revolution, the former dismissed the enterprise as 'Satanic'. In their clamourings, both groups vied with each other; the Protectionists hoped that the structure might be hit by lightning, the Nonconformists prayed that some act of God might smite 'the Monster'. All was to no avail. On the First of May, 1851, the project had been realized. Her Majesty arrived to open the Crystal Palace[1] (Plates XXVI-XXVIII, facing pp. 84, 85, and 92).

[1] There were over three hundred thousand people in the Park—among them Macaulay, who wrote in his journal that night: '[The Crystal Palace] is a most gorgeous sight; vast; graceful; beyond the dreams of Arabian romances. I cannot

XXII. Stanhope Gate, Hyde Park; a water-colour by Decimus Burton c. 1826.

XXIII. Grosvenor Gate, Hyde Park; a water-colour by Decimus Burton, c. 1826.

That morning, from before breakfast, the Queen had been all of a dither. Seldom were Londoners to see her so elated and interested, for this was the triumph of her beloved Albert, 'the most *beautiful* and *imposing* and *touching* spectacle ever seen', 'the *greatest* day in our history'.

After a short sermon by the Archbishop of Canterbury, the 'Hallelujah' chorus was sung—and Handel 'made Englishmen proud of the musical resources of their country', wrote the newspapers with one accord. Yet so many green acres did the iron vaulting cover that the thunderous 'Amen' was nearly lost—albeit those present declared the eye to well recompense the ear for what it missed. Between the pillars and the red hangings, flags on masts had been planted beside palm trees; and beside these had been set the scientific discoveries of four continents. At one end stood a finely carved Amazon by Kiss, at the other a glass fountain played. Looking at the catalogue which had been presented to her, the Queen learnt that the sommerphone was a wind instrument; she grew impatient to see it and the procession formed up. Behind her Lord Anglesey and the Duke of Wellington walked arm-in-arm; they followed Joseph Paxton who—God bless him!—had risen from a common gardener's boy to being the architect of this superb adventure. And now enters the one mystery figure of the occasion.

Dressed in his national costume, a Chinaman pushed his way through the crowd. 'He might possibly be the Emperor,' Lord Play-fair thought. '. . . and we who were in charge of the ceremony did not know where to place his Celestial Highness.' Nor did Her Majesty, Prince Albert or the Lord Chamberlain; nor were any of them quite sure who he was since none of them had ever met the Emperor. So, after a quick consultation, it was decided safest to put him between the Archbishop and the Duke, since, if the Church and the Army were the props of a civilized society, then would not this act also set a precedent in the eyes of the rest of the world and more especially in the Far East? All was ready for the tour of inspection to move off. . . .

think that the Caesars ever exhibited a more splendid spectacle. I was quite dazzled, and I felt as I did on entering St. Peter's.' Then he settled down to finish *Persuasion*: 'I have now read over again all Miss Austen's novels. Charming they are; but I found a little more to criticize than formerly. Yet there are in the world no compositions which approach nearer to perfection.'

'Far from being a Mandarin, he was a mere impostor.' Such would appear to be the verdict of Lytton Strachey. Others report that after the ceremony they traced him to a junk lying on the Thames, which he allowed them to inspect at a shilling a head. History records no more. Yet I am not sure that this same Chinaman does not turn up later in the same year. I base this speculation on Berlioz's diaries.

Berlioz had been appointed a member of the Musical Jury of the Great Exhibition while it was still in the Park. Unlike Haydn, Chopin or Weber, he never suffered the pangs of home-sickness. Instead, he is the perfect example of the man whose index to his character does not lie in his outward features—the massive brow, the grizzly hair or bloodless complexion which suggest an eagle in captivity; rather, there is an inner man who is full of comic humour blended with a sense of the ridiculous. Such was the man who accepted a white surplice and allowed himself to chant the Psalms in St. Paul's with six thousand charity children. But it was not the same man who tottered out of the choir an hour later.

In the pouring rain, he took a boat to Chelsea and returned to his lodgings. There, his guitar offered him no solace, and sleep gave him the slip that night and all the next day. In a complete state of exhaustion, upon the second night, he heard voices singing, 'All People That On Earth Do Dwell' and saw St. Paul's transformed 'into pandemonium and instead of the Archbishop in his pulpit', he saw 'Satan on his throne; in lieu of the thousands of worshippers and children grouped about him, hosts of demons and damned shot their fiery glances from the bosom of the visible darkness, and the iron amphitheatre on which these millions sat vibrated in its entirety in a terrible fashion, pouring out hideous harmonies the while'. He rushed from his room into the streets—only to be pursued by ghoulish figures from the canvases of Doré and Wiertz. As the dawn reddened, he found himself at the gates of the Great Exhibition. Was this the reality of the iron amphitheatre which he had seen in his dream, or was he sleep-walking? As much a mystery exists here as over what ensued.

Apparently, unchecked by any sentry, he found his way to the Bohemian Glass Court, where a solitary sparrow caught his attention, perched between the enormous jaws of a Spanish cannon. Was this some Arabian nightmare, the opulence of the East falling in a profusion of bokhara and silk over gunmetal and girder alike? By day, the building resembled a giant greenhouse; now it seemed more like a birdcage of the gods. Neither he nor the sparrow were alone. There was a soft flutter of feathers over jasmine; he watched a body of brilliant plumage take shape; a Mandarin was dusting a vase. The composer tried to speak, but no words came. His effort was stifled with contempt—yet who could say if the contempt was for his dishevelled appearance, his music or the barbaric bread sandwiches which the Chinese figure proceeded to munch? Had not he met this merchant before? Had not his junk lain in the Thames? Had not perhaps this great roof been his nightly canopy for the past six months? Then the man sighed—and Berlioz thought: he is evidently dreaming 'of his own country ... [and of] succulent shark's fins fried in castor oil ... swallow's nest soup, and the famous woodlouse jam they make so well in Canton'. He could not suppress a yawn; the loss of two days' sleep weighed heavily. 'Ugh! The thought of this uncivil epicure [gave] me nausea and I withdrew.'

Here, then, are the two stories; the first about the Mandarin in the royal procession has acquired the mystique of a legend, whilst the other has slipped by unnoticed. Was it the same Chinaman, or was it the fancy of a tired mind?

In sifting the material, the modern historian may be tempted to think the province nearer the psychiatrist's than his own; in this he will be acting according to his age and time. But the older historian may be less willing to departmentalize his work; if he is a nonagenerian, he may regale the listener with the fireside fact of the 311,731 lb. of Bath buns eaten in the first six months in the Park, or he may recall the pantomime of *Little Miss Muffet* which he saw at Sydenham (with August Manns conducting); it will be his way of saying that with the Crystal Palace era all things were possible. And with this difference of interpretation between the historian of yesterday and today, there is underlined also the distance travelled in a century from Berlioz to Bartok, from the Great Exhibition in Hyde Park to the Festival Hall on the South Bank.

79

VII

THE PROFIT MADE by the World's Fair was £165,000. During its six months' stay in the Park it had become neither a rallying point for malcontents nor had its roof proved porous and its twenty caged green acres been turned to swamp. Those who had prophesied disaster discreetly forgot their earlier views and joined in the national rejoicing. The country's prestige could not have stood higher. The Organizing Committee of the adventure had been invited to Paris and fêted, while the Queen and Prince Consort had made a triumphant progress through the towns north of the Wash. The money had been banked and interest accrued; the art exhibits had been transferred to Marlborough House and public curiosity increased. How canalize the two? In the end, it was decided that the profits should be invested in a museum for South Kensington.

So, in 1857, the South Kensington Museum was opened, and it was in the next year that Frank Buckland, the famous naturalist, delivered his maiden lecture there. His subject was, 'Horn, Hair and Bristles'. Eight years later he was appointed Scientific Referee, and on receiving this appointment he added his own private collection of fish and oyster specimens to that already gathered by the curator. It was not surprising therefore that when it was agreed that the Serpentine should be drained the choice for supervising such a task should fall upon him. Thus it was that on a late sunny autumn morning, he made his way up Exhibition Road towards the Alexandra Gate.

A fisherman from Hammersmith had been engaged and from a rowing boat the initial haul was made. There had been few people in the Park when work began, but the word spread and an audience soon gathered. In less than an hour, 'so many people had assembled, and they pushed down the bank so heavily on us, that it was almost impossible to do any work at all'. As the first catch was drawn nearer the shore, so the sticklebacks began to dance in the air above the net,

XXIV. The Spring Well, Hyde Park; a pen and ink drawing by an unknown artist.

XXV. Hyde Park Corner in the 1840's; a drawing by T. S. Boys and subsequently sold as a lithograph.

'glittering in the sun like a shower of silver spangles'. The performance was met with derision; there was some hooting, a little slow clapping and a good deal of booing. Only the boys, with their empty pickle jars, remained silent. Then, 'Jimmy,' shouted one of them. 'We'd better go home, the gent is killing all the tittlers.'

Three water-carts were used, and as the fish were taken out of the water, so they were dropped into buckets; when all the buckets were filled, the carts left for the Round Pond. In all they made eleven journeys, taking with them over five thousand fish. Most were roach, Prussian and Crucian carp, bream or tench. One eel, one trout and one perch were also netted; but the solitary perch was 'a cripple, for his upper jaw was rounded into a knob like an apple, and his deformed face looked like a pantomime mask'.[1]

If there is something humorous in the description, it has too something about it that is ghoulish. As the water slowly sank down the forty foot delve, so a human chain was made and it must have been a strange sight to see the old Hammersmith fisherman wading lower and lower into the mud. Nor did the day's work pass 'without incident'. At one moment, just after the perch had passed from hand to hand to the bucket, Buckland had to give the fellow 'a good pull . . . and he came suddenly out of the mud with a flop like a cork from a wine bottle'. This was to prevent him 'from floundering about like a giant hippopotamus'.

Again, here is the note of pantomime, but it is pantomime in the old style when the curtain rose and fell on a harlequinade; and the clowns in a harlequinade with their chalked faces and currant eyes can be as terrifying to a child as the albino. For the aim of a mask, or a clown's make-up, is to place an emphasis on a particular feature—a Cyrano nose or goitrous eyes that revolve like tennis balls. Or with the albino, what so often frightens the child is the unexpected pinkness mixed with an almost other-worldly whiteness. In fiction, the albino character is frequently a symbol of evil. 'They are a disorder'—and the term disorder is closely allied with another, formlessness. Plato speaks of a

[1] No fishing is allowed in the Serpentine today—only boating and bathing. In August each year there is a rowing regatta. See tailpieces to this and the previous chapter for a happy memory of the 1850s (pp. 46 and 100). Frequently however anglers re-assert their old rights!

realization that 'evil hovers of necessity around mortal nature and this earthly sphere'. Grotesque ugliness can attract like the bizarre—as in the case of the jellyfish or octopus. With women this characteristic is sometimes called *belle laide*. But in the case of a deformity such as that of the crippled perch, the beauty is outweighed by the ugliness. What strikes terror in children in these instances is the primordial chaos insurgent beneath the order superimposed. A gnarled oak may inspire a sonnet or a painter's admiration—but then it is immobile: were it to come alive it might well be thought an ogre—and in pantomime it is a popular trick for a witch to hide in a tree while the heroine, looking for somewhere to rest, suddenly finds that the harmless branches have ensnared her within their power.

The whimsy of James Barrie draws close, and it is worth contrasting how the Serpentine which to Buckland was a sheet of fifty acres of water becomes for Barrie 'a lovely lake . . . with a drowned forest at the bottom of it. If you peer over the edge', he adds, 'you can see all the trees growing upside down, and they say at night there are also drowned stars in it.'

This may have been written as fancy—and yet it is fancy backed up subconsciously by history. For when there were eleven marshy pools here, the monks had trees felled so that their trunks might be lashed into causeways; many of their stumps now lie embedded forty feet beneath the water, while at the east end of the lake, there reads this inscription on an urn: 'A supply of water by conduit from this spot was granted to the Abbey of Westminster with the manor of Hyde by King Edward the Confessor. The manor was resumed by the Crown in 1536 but the springs as a head were preserved to the Abbey by the charter of Queen Elizabeth in 1560.'

Today, from the Lansbury lido, goggle-swimming makes it possible to explore the remains of this underwater forest; 'frog feet' make a reality of what to Barrie may have been either a lucky guess, or a form of whimsy. For to dive beneath the surface, leaving the laughter of the banks behind, is to enter a graveyard of infants' skeletons left by the Eighteenth Century. The experience is bizarre—a sudden linking of the quick and the dead, recalling the novels of Pierre Loti and the Turkish whores who offer themselves to clients on tombstones so that their lovers shall never forget that in the midst of life they are in death. This may sound illogical—although in another sense it is extremely logical. It is part of the illogicality of truth made logical by paradox—as for instance when the Royal Humane Society decided to build their life-boat house[1] (Plate XXVII, facing p. 85) just in front of the cockpit where duels used to be fought. But to hark back to Buckland. . . .

In the reign of Henry VIII, the King's hunting grounds had stretched unbroken from Westminster to Hampstead Heath; right into the Eighteenth Century, deer had been hunted (they were only finally removed from Hyde Park in 1831), and on that morning in the mid-century when the Serpentine was dredged a few masks and antlers were found. A question mooted—in fact raised at one of Buckland's lectures—had been whether park deer who were conscious of 'the difference between the fowling piece and the rifle when in the keeper's hands, had sufficient thinking power to look up a tree when their enemy was concealed therein'. At the time he had not been able to give a direct answer, but in working towards an answer he decided that their nostrils were more receptive than their eyes. 'The deer trusts more to his senses of smell and hearing than he does to sight.' For 'the eye itself is very small, and only weighs one ounce; the lens is ex-ceedingly transparent and crystalline, and the retina painted a beautiful green colour, not unlike that of the sea-mouse; the optic nerve is about the size of a large wheat-straw'. Again, 'we now come to the nose. The nostril itself will admit the top of a forefinger easily. The bone which covers the nasal organ is exceedingly thin. Upon taking it off I find a most wonderful apparatus for enabling the deer to smell. It consists of two pear-shaped bones, the structure of which is like the thinnest film of wax.' There follows the summing-up: 'Upon these bones the delicate nerves of smell are outspread, so as to become cognisant of the slightest scent which may be wafted in the air' and from which 'I at once make bold to state that we human beings cannot possibly have any notion of the acute power of smell possessed by a deer. . . . I think he seldom, if ever, looks above him, because (except when the

[1] The Serpentine Road on this northern bank has running on its far side a stretch of gravel mixed with tan laid for horse-riders. It is sometimes referred to as the Ladies' Mile. No motor-traffic is allowed along here. The lifeboat house itself, known officially as the 'Royal Humane Society Receiving House', was built in 1854.

sportsman perches himself in a tree) there is nothing particular to see.'
Pictures abound of Charles II up a tree, while the soldiers go about
'beneath him looking in every direction save the right one. "Eyes up"
is an unknown command. It is not the deer alone leave people sitting in
trees undisturbed. . . .'

Yet, in this conclusion, Buckland was far from sentimentalizing
animals, or equating them with human beings. His descriptions have a
scientific accuracy; the ascetic pleasure they provide is incidental—
rather as a knowledge of the stresses of poetry is incidental to an
appreciation of it. (Among modern writers of this century, W. N. P.
Barbellion and Geoffrey Grigson run him closest.) He would have been
appalled at the Dogs' Cemetery which was opened by the Victoria
Gate during 1880, the year of his death. There, until the first World
War, pet dogs, cats and birds were buried. Their grave-stones remain
—about three hundred in all. One rather nauseating epitaph reads:

IN LOVING MEMORY OF
PUSKIN
MY GENTLE FRIEND
AND COMPANION FOR ELEVEN YEARS
SO SADLY MISSED

. . .

SLEEP LITTLE ONE SLEEP
REST GENTLY THY HEAD
AS EVER THOU DIDST AT MY FEET
AND DREAM THAT I AM ANEAR

I FAITHFULLY LOVED AND CARED
FOR YOU LIVING · I THINK
WE SHALL SURELY MEET AGAIN

The names of some of the dogs are significant: 'Little Lord Quex',
'Dear Pepys', and 'My Little Dorrit'. One tombstone bears a Shakes-
pearean line quite wittily transposed:

After life's fitful slumber, he sleeps well.

One remembers the Queen's Boz who was made immortal as he
lay in bronze, wreathed in flowers, upon the dinner-table at Windsor.
Will the names of pets again take a literary turn? 'Lucky Jim', 'Crouch-
back', or 'Eustace and Hilda'. . . .

XXVI. The Crystal Palace from the South Side, a lithograph, one of 'seven picturesque views', by Philip Brannan, 1851.
(*Note the houses of Kensington Gore on the left*)

XXVII. The Crystal Palace from the North Bank of the Serpentine; also by Philip Brannan.

VIII

A T THE SOUTH end of the Wellington Drive, facing Achilles, was erected a statue of Lord Byron. The poet is seated upon a rock and beside him is his collie. The bronze was cast in 1880 by R. C. Belt—though Trelawny found in it no resemblance to his friend.[1] Augustus Hare too dismisses it as 'feeble' and more recently F. R. Banks has called it 'inadequate'. The judgments may stand.

Naturally those who disliked the statue could blame it on the change of Government. The Whigs were a useful scapegoat and as Gladstone took over from Disraeli, so Art slipped in its own revolution and legislated for it. The 'greenery yallery of the Grosvenor Gallery' allowed canary coloured garments to blend with undreamed-of shades of grass: for every model that had posed for a canvas there walked away a dozen imitators within a few hours of seeing it. Frivolous bonnets sprouted from a mantle that might have been drawn by Dürer; billowing cloaks that might have surrounded a Mater Dolorosa hung beside magenta striped hoods. Beauty was the key-word; 1880 was a magic date. A small boy of seven in his velveteen breeches was to recall a decade later how bank clerks returning home from the City would declare the poetry of the Underground Railway from London Bridge superior to that from Sloane Square to Notting Hill Gate. Yet this is to forestall 'the incomparable Max'. . . .

The magic date that he circled with his pen was of beauty made brilliant in its own halo rather than in a spotlight. Lady Campbell at Coome Wood liked Shakespeare to be presented pastorally; her players were amateurs lest her audience might have been lured to foresake their

[1] On the far side of the road, a few hundred yards to the north and opposite Grosvenor Gate, is a fountain with a boy and a dolphin. It is the work of Alexander Munro, one of the early members of the pre-Raphaelites. Another fountain, a Gothic drinking-fountain, stands just to the west of Marble Arch, inside the Park. It was given to Londoners by the Maharaja Merza Vijiaram Gajapatriam Manca Sooltan Behadoar of Vijianagram in 1867.

tied-back skirts, black jerseys and Zulu hats, or their escorts to abandon their light frock coats and light top hats with one black band. Beauty was its own profession; acting a pleasant pastime—while stage life was something quite removed from both. It was assumed that a taste for the Beautiful went with a taste for the Intellectual in conversation. Lady Freake in her *tableaux* at Cromwell House presented Mrs. Cornwallis West as Amy Robstart, while Mrs. Langtry appeared stepping across an artificial brook 'in the pink kirtle of Effie Deans'; and to have mentioned the Jersey Lily is to understand the difference between these *tableaux* or amateur theatricals and the professional theatre.

On the stage, she never commanded a big following; her perform-ances did not drag tears from the policeman standing at the back of the pit. Rather it was in Rotten Row as she passed that rangers would take off their hats and young aesthetics, holding lilies, jump on chairs the better to see her. It was here that her beauty was unrivalled and that she brought into fashion the Langtry-hood, -bonnet and -shoe.

'The Lily is so tiresome. She won't do what I tell her,' said Oscar Wilde once. 'How wrong,' asked Graham Robertson, who a few years back had nearly fallen under the Barnes omnibus in his excitement to see her. 'Yes,' murmured Wilde, 'I assure her that she owes it to herself and to us to drive daily through the Park dressed entirely in black in a black victoria drawn by black horses and with "Venus Annodomini" emblazoned on her black bonnet in dull sapphires.'

Yet had she done so, it would only have been to imitate Mrs. Wheeler, who always 'appeared in black'. As a boy I remember hearing the title 'Jersey Lily' and wondering to whom it referred. I began to associate it with another story—but which I am unable to verify.

In the last century, Lord Dorchester, despite repeated protests by the Commissioners of Woods and Forests, insisted on keeping a cow and allowing her to graze in the Park. No deputation could take from him what he believed was his common right—and until his dying day a cow was taken out of his stable each morning, led across the lane, and tethered in the long grass. The 'Jersey Lily' was a phrase I had always associated with milkmaids and I was surprised to see in a book of theatrical memoirs a writer praise Mrs. Langtry's Audrey, the apple-cheeked wench in *As You Like It*, above all her other rôles. There was no artifice, no coarse guffawing over a property turnip, no excessive business. It was simply beauty unadorned—which is perhaps why she never drew packed houses; there was not that necessary exaggeration which appears so natural behind the footlights and distinguishes the great actress. Instead, packed houses were drawn by Katie Vaughan or Nellie Farren. Nightly, amid the gilt encrustations, ornate boxes and velvet tassels, they filled the Gaiety Theatre to capacity. There arose the cult of the Mashers as in the Eighteenth Century there had been the cult of the Macaronies.

There are two possible derivations of the name: *ma chère*, a term of endearment used by the young men of the period towards barmaids, or the line from a chorus of a song that went:

I'm the slashing, dashing, mashing Montmorency of the day.

Occasionally, in the early summer months when the sun-blinds on the verandahs were still down, there would stroll through Grosvenor Gate flaxen haired Mashers, as ready to lean upon their canes to bow to those dressed in the confections of Worth, as once, a tasselled cane ever ready to lift the hat, the Macaronies would specially salute all those who had discarded the hoop for the trailing gown. Again, whereas in East Carriage Drive the Macaronies had their feet bound as small as possible and their shoes crested with diamonds, so in Wellington Drive the Mashers aimed to make their feet look as narrow as two black needles. Larwood who disapproved of this affectation, which coincided more or less with the publication of his *Story of the London Parks* (1881), omits all mention of it: he claims sanctuary in 1825, considering all that followed 'too near to contemporary history' to allow him to be honest without causing offence. Yet undetected one judgment did slip in when unsuspectingly he compared the Macaroni ladies to those of his own day—and added: 'Thus it has ever been. Old abominations of fashion every now and again crop up . . . to shame our boasts of having grown wiser than our ancestors.'

This is a moralizing that has been pursued by numerous other observers in Hyde Park—although what is perhaps less remarked is the

way in which certain parks become stamped with certain characteristics and retain them through the ages. For example, the tub-thumpers
at Marble Arch might be described today as the nervous tics of society
—a judgment, so marked by the recent impact of psychology on
language, that it savours of the case-book. Quarter of a century ago,
when sociology rather than psychology was in the ascendant, 'poor
sod' was a term often levelled at those soap-box orators who came
either to promote hunger marches or win arms for Spain. Half a
century ago, although the 'Nineties were over, there still lingered the
phrase 'the Don Fantasticos of words'.

These changes of opinion are reflections of public outlook—though
common to all three is an attitude that a psychiatrist nowadays might
summarize as 'a quaranteening of the speaker'. For the speaker is
essentially a performer like the actor, and, like the actor, a distance
must be maintained between him and his audience. He can make his
platform either a pedestal or a pulpit. A few, with coarsely matted
locks and long oval faces, sometimes see their rôles as clowns; they
provide the coconuts on the shies, the buskers whose nightly routine for
the gallery queues is brought into the Park on Sundays. Yet a bye-
law prevents them from begging; instead a nervous tic keeps them
going as they alternate between texts from the Bible or Othello's
speech to the Senate, or, with a quick twist of a hat, make Nelson out of
Napoleon.

A speaker of quite another and individual character—who has
written his memoirs—was Bonar Thompson. In a black hat, he would
discourse on Anything; but what was even more of a feat he would
also talk on Nothing. His style was a cross between Shavian syllogism
and Chestertonian paradox, but Chestertonian paradox of the young
G.K. before he grew repetitious. Bonar Thompson was probably the
most professional speaker the Park has ever had because whereas the
political parties frequently pay their speakers, he relied entirely on
voluntarary contributions. Yet these, as he would explain, were
illegal to accept on this side of the railings—though there was nothing
against a florin changing hands on the pavement beyond. Then would
come the battle-cry, 'To the Gates, Ladies and Gentlemen', and digging
in their pockets a few faithful stragglers would follow this hawk-like

figure to the street. In his book, he suggested as his epitaph, 'The Collection Was Not Enough'.

The young Chesterton once said, 'Every splintered fraction of a sect finds a voice here.' I recall a German publisher telling me after the war how his attention had wandered from Bonar Thompson to a louder, more raucous speaker who was proposing the instant dissolution of the monarchy. Suddenly he became conscious of a policeman watching; he waited for him to intervene, but was surprised to see him turning towards the road. There, he heard him say to a motorist parked at the side: 'Would you mind lowering your wireless, sir? The people can't hear.'

Maybe this was a typical foreigner's story, and undoubtedly it would be met in some circles with a smart cynicism; I would be reminded how unfairly some émigrés were imprisoned in 1939 and I would be informed of the present cases of police corruption. Instead, I prefer to take the story at its face value. Orators' Corner is a safety valve in the national life. Communism may be expounded as well as answered by a hundred different voices belonging to a hundred different sects in a hundred different ways. But the fact remains that it can be expounded; also its exposition, in a place of so many other shades of conflicting opinion, offers a lesson in tolerance. A parson may be ragged by the spectators and he will take it in good faith; if some jester asks if the Thirty-Nine Articles are related to the Thirty-Nine Steps, he will not necessarily grow hot around the collar. Of if a heckler attacks a young Tory, such a candidate will not grow antagonistic if there follows an exchange of repartee over the word 'right'; it is all a part of the fun of electioneering. Yet if the same heckler walks away to the next pitch and begins weighing in with quips about the Gospel according to Marx, he will find that he is up against quite an alien kind of mentality.[1] Nor does this have anything to do with the Russian people, since temperamentally the British and Russians are not so unalike: on the contrary, it is precisely the inflexibility of

[1] Incidentally, in August 1958, Harry Diamond who usually wears a raincoat, smokes his own home-made cigarettes and has been speaking weekly for five years, gave this advice to potential hecklers: 'Get near enough to the speaker to be able to shout him down—and far away enough so that he can't hit you!' Then he added: 'I like the crackpots best. They're more exciting than television.'

Communists to be able to laugh at themselves that has so often thwarted their efforts. Hyde Park offers them a double trap, because should these English Commissars come to power, the freedom which they now use they could only then abuse. For such always is the price of political fanaticism.

No less to be avoided is religious fanaticism. Every so often it shows its head in the form of periodical purity purges by over-pious bodies. But their campaigns are not blessed (if blessed at all) with much under-standing of human nature. For pimping and accosting have always been a part of the London scene: at Marble Arch and around its green fringes they merely exist more openly than elsewhere. This is nothing new and there have been many ballads sung about it down the centuries. One Restoration version begins with this explanatory note: 'News from Hyde Park; or, A very merry Passage which hapnd betwixt a North Country Gentleman and a Very Gaudy Gallant Lady of pleasure, whom he took up in the Parke, and conducted her (in her own coach) home to her Lodgings, and what chanced there, if you'll venter attention the song will declare.' The tune goes to that of 'The Crost Couple'.

Against such happenings, fire and brimstone have been constantly called down; by different preachers, London has been compared to Babylon; Pompeii; Hawaii. Yet what these preachers so often forget is that extreme piety can be equally unhealthy, and that religious love (in excess) can be closely allied to (excessive) sexual love. For when a man has found his salvation, his next desire is to find his Eve and Paradise. (At the time of the Roundheads, for instance, the Lady Eleanor was quite convinced that Hyde Park was Paradise.)[1] So it is that when these 'revival' movements are led by women, carnal loves becomes taboo and spiritual mating the accepted rule, whereas when these movements are run by men, the theocratic impulse turns in the opposite direction, and polygamy becomes the accepted order of the day. In both cases, but with a different understanding, a supernaturalized sex is sought in a supernaturalized social order; and in this unnatural state, bordering on the edges of hysteria, all kinds of cankers far worse than prostitution may grow and fester beneath the surface.

[1] See p. 57.

On Good Friday, 1954, Billy Graham, the American Evangelist, moved from the boxing basilica that he had made of Harringay Arena to the Park. In the wide open spaces, he was careful neither to gesticulate wildly nor rave about sins of omission or the wrath of the Lord. In his dove-grey suit, on the springy soles of his crepe shoes, he moved about as a boxer; there was always a hint of the brooding champion. 'We will pray now . . .' and he began with naming the Royal Family. 'Every head bent. I ask everyone to keep as still as possible. The movement of a single person may distract thousands.' The thousands who came to hear him created a record and if this was 'revivalism', as some newspapers insisted, then it was 'revivalism' of quite another, subtler form to the vagaries preached by Moody and Sankey, Torrey-Alexander or Aimée Macpherson.

Curiously enough, this kind of 'revivalism' hovers much nearer Prince Monolulu—though his texts are betting slips, and his appearances, alas, are much fewer than they were wont to be. In his sweeping clothes, crowned with a most brilliant plumage of feathers, he is quite literally the most colourful speaker on this Corner. When he is in full flight, I have often wondered how deep one would have to prick the dark skin to start the jungle-beat of the tom-toms; the trembling, weeping, swooning; the jittering of feet, or the flapping of arms like wings. For when he has his audience in thrall, they not only believe that they might follow him to the ends of the moon but that any instant they may become airborne and do so.

This gallery of speakers cannot be closed without mention of a dear friend of the Park, the late Fr. Vincent McNabb, the saintly Dominican. One of his Sunday retorts is still treasured by many. 'What would you do if your wife put poison in your coffee?' a woman pestered for the umpteenth time. 'Madam,' he replied, 'if you were my wife, I'd drink it.' As he stood in his pulpit, his habit billowing in the breeze, his body had the quality of an ancient tree—it was all roots and yet there was nothing gnarled or twisted about it. His approach was direct and he was the kind of man about whom legends develop, because there is a sense in which legends reach out beyond the truth.

A charwoman of my acquaintance saved her sixpences to buy him a carrying-case for the Extreme Unction oils. Each morning she would attend the six o'clock mass at Saint Dominic's Church, Haverstock Hill. Years later as he lay dying, prayers were asked of the congregation. One morning, arriving early before the doors were opened, she saw a lark soaring over the Heath and her thoughts flew at once to Father Vincent. At that very moment, it was announced afterwards, he had died.

Now, sometimes when I walk to Orators' Corner, looking towards Cumberland Gate (which used to face the old Tyburn toll-gate), I can see the starlings that have flown from Kensington Gardens roosting in the plane trees. Behind their gaunt winter traceries stands a copy of Constantine's marble arch: the mark of an Emperor's triumphs, Nash's replica was first set before Buckingham Palace until in 1851 it was removed to its new site. In the summer, however, along this vista, the line of its Corinthian columns becomes lost in the waving green; and as the evening draws in, so the carrara grows luminous in all the different gradations of light, while only the birds remain to mock the day's passing traffic, the sound and fury of all the debate and argument of Marble Arch Corner.[1]

[1] There are schemes afoot to cut off twenty-one acres of the Park between here and Hyde Park Corner. Such vandalism has been gallantly opposed by John Betjeman and many others; but as yet all is in the balance. The pretext is the heavy traffic in Park Lane. There are also distant threats—on the same pretext—to the green acres around Victoria Gate and Queen's Gate. There are, however, some more sensible plans to build underground garages at strategic points round Kensington Gardens and Hyde Park. A new underground entrance at Knightsbridge called Edinburgh Gate and opened in April, 1959, is the most recent of these developments.

XXVIII. Looking over the Dam (or Dell) at the Crystal Palace; also by Philip Brannan.

IX

'I CALL THESE MY chickens, and I'm obliged to come every day to feed them,' said a paralytic, white-haired old man to W. H. Hudson as he scattered a bag of crumbs for a school of sparrows. The place was the Dell, behind the Serpentine (Plate XXVIII, facing p. 92); the time, the middle 'Nineties—a peak period for both *The Savoy* and *The Yellow Book*. Often these *fin de siècle* publications are dismissed as decadent simply because they appeared at the end of an era, whereas in actual fact they were nothing of the kind. If Dowson, Ella D'Arcy and Richard le Gallienne were contributors, so too were Shaw, George Gissing and H. G. Wells. With Hudson also, a strong social bias tempered his thought: 'A field-naturalist is an observer of everything he sees—from men to an ant on a plant.' The world of nature for him was subject 'to the mind's projection', so that the struggle of a bedraggled blackbird with a relentless chaffinch might begin a train of reflection leading from a discourse on the morality of war to a study of the optic nerve, or the curious friendship of pumas towards the human species.

Of all birds, the sparrow is the most perky; the colour of the City, he is the first Cockney amongst them.[1] A good errand boy is said to be 'as sharp as a sparrow', and a deserted railway siding, or the sad façade of Working Men's Clubs, seem incomplete without their urchin-calls.

Hudson was one of those gifted observers who do not seek, but find: to say that many of his findings were fortuitous is to misunderstand that he was conditioned by nature to discover precisely what he did find. 'Only Verrochio could portray such innocence' is a cliché of art criticism—yet a cliché that is heard often enough about the copy of the

---

[1] A century ago, Phil. Robinson described him as 'the gamin of birds—chief vagabond of the air', and went on: 'This Bohemian communist has broken through —worn out—the resentment of man; we no longer resist his intrusions or retaliate for his rapine.'

winged cherub from the Palazzo Vecchio,[1] which stands between a fine bronze Dian by Countess Gleichen, supported by four caryatids, and the Dell.

What Hudson saw, others were less willing to see—and hence the continual rejection of his early essays. Neither *The Yellow Book* nor *The Savoy* found that he could provide what they were looking for. Nor were his early books successful. When Frank Swinnerton was a reception-clerk at Dents, he recalls a meeting with a tall, thin man whose overcoat almost reached his heels; whose tanned shrunken face 'resembled a bird . . . but . . . had not the malignance of a hawk or the solemnity of an owl or the satisfied memory of a parrot'. Indeed, what struck Swinnerton was the stillness of his movements; his power of merging into a landscape; his ability to watch birds, ducks and rabbits by the hour—as indeed, unobserved one day at the Dell, he also watched two labourers, with tired, dusty features, produce from their pockets bread and meat, saved from the midday meal and carefully wrapped in newspaper. Then one spoke: 'Come on, mate, they've had it all, and now let's go home and see what the missus has got for our tea.' And home he saw them trudge, 'with hearts refreshed and lightened, no doubt, to be succeeded by others and still others, London workmen and their wives and children, until the sun had set and all the birds were gone'.

In 1922 he died, and London paid its formal tribute—a sorry tribute. Before a narrow stretch of dead water, set between privets, there reads an inscription: 'This Sanctuary for Birds is Dedicated to the Memory of W. H. Hudson—Writer and Field-Naturalist.' At the back, in the middle of a flat stone screen, is a freize by Epstein. It represents Rima, a semi-human embodiment of the forest-spirit which appears in *Green Mansions* (1904). There is too an eagle which H. J. Massingham believed to be a mocking-bird portrait of the author himself. 'When I used to go and see him . . . , it was like taking one of the hunched eagles at the Zoo out of his cage for an airing.' Apart from Massingham's censures, there have been many other criticisms of this work.

---

[1] In Florence itself silver copies of this cherub are sold as bottle-stoppers in the market. Which reminds me too that some Italian bus drivers have a habit of describing their own Pincio Gardens as 'Roma's Hyde Park'!

Speaking for the common man, Arthur Mee declares the sculptor's 'birds . . . were never in any realm of Nature', and goes on to protest that Rima's hands resemble claws; he adds nothing of the ugliness of her corrugated hair. Certainly, remembering Epstein's pair of marble doves, or his Black Madonna in Cavendish Square, the Park freize is a total failure. He sought, but did not find—the one piece of really dead work, which is perhaps the price that any great sculptor must pay. For, unmarked by any plaque, it is the Dell which remains Hudson's most fitting monument. There, to all the animal kingdom (save 'stoats, publishers, weasels and ferrets') he could project his sympathy. There, day after day he would stand till dusk fell and he must needs retreat to his boarding house to which his manuscripts returned with the regularity of homing pigeons. There, other writers may still stand, watching pigeons—and take heart.

X

A T THE FAR END of the Dell is a pedestal supporting a vase. An inscription on one side records how a supply of water was granted to Westminster Abbey by Edward the Confessor, and on the other a tablet commemorates the old conduit house which stood on this spot. In 1861, drainage cut off the supply from the spring, and what had appeared in the Eighteenth Century as something of a natural ruin became a century later no more than scattered stones on a hill suggesting the near vicinity of a quarry. However, east of the Albert Gate where the shops straggle to an end, stands another conduit house—the last relic of Elizabethan architecture in the Park. A few yards back from the main road, grown over by long, trailing ivy, this is a building without eyes: a heavily studded door guards the entrance to the subterranean channels that are the underground veins of the Westbourne. One tributary, on its way to the Thames, is piped a few feet above the passengers who wait daily on Sloane Square Station. These secret channels are reminders both of the Knightsbridge Mill (Plate XV, facing p. 53) and the eleven pools of Hyde Manor that brought more than lenten fare to many a royal and ecclesiastical table.

Today the scene has changed, the landscape altered; but the differences are no more than overlays.

Of the marshes, where razor-edged bulrushes and fat-leaved scurvy grass used to offer a covert to the hawk or heron, smooth lawns have been made. On Bird Island alone (a few feet from the northern shore of the Serpentine) does a hint remain of the earlier lie of the land. Again, on the crests of hills once crowned by forests and now, as at the Dell, made into semi-rocky promontories,[1] in place of the wild boar or the musk-ox, butterflies and lizards disport themselves. For such always is the advance and retreat of nature. When Frank Buckland wrote of the sensitive pear-shaped nostrils of deer, centuries of civiliza-

[1] These megaliths at the Dell come from Liskeard in Cornwall.

tion separated him from Paleolithic Man; in the wide interim, men's nostrils had narrowed in proportion as their need to hunt by scent had grown less. So also with their ears (Swinnerton remarks how W. H. Hudson's ears stuck out from under his black felt hat). It may be a far cry from the savage in his cave scraping the gristle from a deer-skin to the pursuit of the great crested eagle to provide hats for Mrs. Buckland or Mrs. Hudson, but it is by such parallels that one age is put in mind of another; and parallels as these come easily in parks.

Boys with boot-lace ties, talking loudly and gesticulating as their hands half cuffed in nylon glitter with heavy signet rings, carry with them a feeling of the Renaissance. Or at Orators' Corner, modern girls, swinging along in groups with cropped hair and dressed in slacks, recall Pepys: 'I [saw ladies] with coats and doublets with deep skirts, just for all the world like mine, and their doublets buttoned up the breasts, with periwigs and with hats, so that, only for a long petti-coat dragging under their men's coats, nobody would take them for women in any point whatever.' These are the comparisons of fashion—the necessary stock in trade of each chronicler of his day. Yet there are other comparisons which are closer to race structure or memory.

That immorality leads to further immorality is a well-known axiom: but excessive morality can also produce immorality, for excess goes against nature—and as early as 1787 the Society for the Suppression of Vice, founded by Robert Wilberforce, was campaigning against 'the lungs of London' being turned into 'the lusts of London'. Yet this kind of campaigning has always been to shut the other eye; enthusiasm for revivalism has often run to excess, expressing itself in the open fields of parklands—as did Puritanism, another parallel. For it should be remembered that sexual attraction is as much a natural instinct as virginity's defence is instinctive, and the desire to destroy innocence can be as strong as the desire to preserve it. Rules or social taboos have to be made; and it was any neglect of these taboos or social rules that led in Edwardian times to the term 'of not knowing the ropes'. So it is that right down to the present, the Park has retained its social hours as well as seasons. If no longer Augusts spent upon the Moors cause shutters to be drawn in Lancaster Gate or Belgravia, then that is because these large houses have been broken down into flats; in place of the old, new snobberies have developed.

In England, at this moment, it is the women's weekly papers that have the really mammoth circulations. Constantly the girls who model for them are photographed against the Rennie's Serpentine Bridge,[1] or Magazine[2] on the north bank; and a study of these photographs and the stories which are sandwiched between them show that these publications are geared for a class of women to whom the dresses worn by these models are, with an exertion, just within financial reach: their public is principally the typist who hopes to be a private secretary or the private secretary who hankers after being an executive in advertising. Frequently, in Christmas numbers, their pages abound with tips for a fiancée who is about to stay with her prospective in-laws and wants to know what are the correct things to do, say and give (the general assumption is always that the man is slightly richer.)[3] So if the Park presents, as it does to every generation, a 'ring' or centre of change, then the wind prevailing now points not so much to a decrease in the ancestral families as the emergence of a whole social middle *bloc* that assesses its position by its spending habits. These might be called the new gatherers; those below, the sowers. Thus, in a curious way at one level, the structure of society is simplifying; and the current division—if the comparison is not stretched too far—recalls the mediaeval world.

At Hyde Park Corner, inside the gates, there was originally a cakehouse and later an apple-stall; both have been replaced by a sweet and paper-stall. Here, on a summer's afternoon, can be watched a parade more telling than any Easter Parade. As feet bound to look like black needles had been the cult of the Mashers, so now black boot-lace ties

[1] Built by the brothers Sir John and George Rennie in 1826.

[2] This used to be called the Guard House—and is still so named on some maps. It was built in the 1760s, but was remodelled in the mid-1820s by Decimus Burton. He was also responsible for the Grosvenor Gate Lodge (Plate XXIII, facing p. 77), Stanhope Gate Lodges (Plate XXII, facing p. 76), Cumberland Gate Lodge and the Lodge west of his Hyde Park Corner screen.

[3] The basic discussion on U and Non-U behaviour had appeared in *Woman* and *Woman's Own* long before the subject had reached more intellectual organs such as *Encounter* or *The Sunday Times*. But less technical and more practical language was used.

XXX. 'Police Waiting for the Reform Meeting'; a contemporary engraving from the *Illustrated London News*, 18th May, 1867.

XXXI. 'Grenadier Guards waiting for the Reform Meeting'; a contemporary engraving from the *Illustrated London News*, 18th May, 1867

have become the uniform of the Teddy Boys. The monk's hood that inspired the Langtry-cap re-appears in the contemporary capuchine; or the head-dress with plumes which superceded the coal scuttle bonnet, is returning—only the plumes are much diminished in height than when they were first worn as a tribute to the Volunteers. The style, *ventum textile* of the late Eighteenth Century, was referred to as 'aerial'; a modern firm of jewellers have put on the market a series of paste brooches in the shape of television masts. It was the Duchess of Bedford riding in the Row, in a blue habit trimmed with white, that prompted George II to introduce these colours for his naval officers; in rejoicings after Cup Finals, sailor caps now invite fellow supporters to 'Steal A Kiss'.

Against a backcloth of Romano's at the Gaiety, a down-at-heel playboy would step forward and sing:

> The other day at tea,
> Baron Rothschild said to me,
> 'Tom, I wonder what it *feels* like to be poor?'

At this Corner, these lines hold a special poignance. For as five o'clock tolls the beginning of the rush hour, so the new gatherers and sowers disperse through the Park: the exempt are the few whose family fortunes have not yet been absorbed in death duties, or those to whom five strikes only in the morning when the gates open, revealing in the green slopes all the promise of green pastures. Yet there was a time when between the rush-hour and dawn, a constant vigil was kept in these fields for enemy planes: all through the long suspense of darkness, time burnt in fingers testing range-finders; in the molten mouths of a hundred guns; in the burning clock towers of London. Once, after a terrible searing flash, I heard a bombadier shout, 'Lumme, Achilles is bleeding'.

The poetry of the moment was lost in the barrage that followed. But in retrospect this could have been a heightened moment such as Blake might have known; nor is the parallel out of context here. For wandering on these slopes, what strange apocalyptic visions may have filled his mind—visions that in his paintings almost seem to foreshadow the explosion of some hydrogen bomb. A statue of Achilles bleeding perhaps makes easier a belief in the arrival of Elias in a fiery chariot; or the attention paid to radio-active dust in an atomic age, perhaps offers an explanation of the dead resurrecting—for nothing dies, no voice is wholly lost but it returns. Truths lie about like straws—to be snatched or blown away. . . .

Beyond the 1828 screen of Decimus Burton, with its triple entrance into Hyde Park, straw used to be laid to soften the sound of the late horse-drawn traffic as it rumbled past St. George's Hospital towards Piccadilly, Kensington or Victoria; and sometimes at night one is still reminded of the practice. In the earlier hours as a lorry roars north, scattering a few straws, so once more the hush of the countryside envelops the sleeping city; the silence becomes emphasized, and the wide stretch of tarmac, between the Ionic columns with their warm glow of mother-of-pearl and the quiet luminosity that radiates from Constitution Arch, diminishes to no more than a moonlit path leading across a track of open ground to a Green Park.

THE HOLDER OF THIS CARD WILL BE REQUIRED,

ON ITS FIRST PRODUCTION, TO FURNISH HIS

ADDRESS TO MR. MANN.

No. 337

Reverse of Serpentine Season ticket.

PART III

GREEN PARK

GREEN PARK

I

THE DARK OAK and the paler ash, the grey willow and the white poplar, are the trees that first made Green Park out of a barren soil of 'drie ditch bankes about Pikadilla'. Here Gerarde, the botanist, later wandered, finding bugloss and ox-tongue; here, in the same reign of Elizabeth, children would come bird-nesting, cutting across the sheep-tracks that skirted the royal farm in St. James's Fields. Shortly after Charles II had ascended the throne, he had these Fields enclosed by a brick wall as far north as the Exeter Road—the additional enclosure being called by some an Upper St. James's Park. Previously, when this land had been made up of two shallow hills, with herons sweeping over its marshy fens that lay in the dip, the slow rising western escarpment had been known as Deer Park; but now the new Monarch referred to it in State Papers as 'a deer harbour', while contemporary chroniclers—notably Strype in his 'continuation[s] of Stow'—spoke generally of St. James's being 'much improved and enlarged . . . *as far as Hyde Park*'. No statement could have led to more topographical confusion.

Only by comparing Norden's plan of 1596 with those of the Stuart cartographers does it become apparent that no change was made to the boundaries of the existing St. James's Park. The southern wall remains the same and Rosamond's Pond in all maps is plotted the same distance from St. James's Palace; again, the buildings of Whitehall show that there could have been no further development to the east. The thirty-six acres, which the King joined as an upper half to his existing Park (see end of chapter, p. 134), have today been increased to fifty-three. In the interim, they have become individually known as Green Park.

The change in name is hard to date. A story popular amongst taxi drivers, and inherited from the cabbies, is that the Park is called Green simply because it is without flowers. Yet this is not strictly true—although walking from the Ritz Hotel to St. George's Hospital[1] (along the former Exeter Road) it is easy to see how the story has grown. Certainly, there are no formal flower-beds as there are in the other royal parks—but there are nonetheless some narrow beds running along the fences of the Queen's Walk. Other writers, with more imagination than attention to facts, have thought the title may have sprung from the surname of a head keeper or ranger; but a study of these appointments during the last four centuries reveals no such clue. A last century song rhapsodizes about 'the grass all around'—and here is a possible derivation, linking as it does the day of the cabbies to the time when a small, homelier Buckingham House fitted the mood of a portly Sovereign as he leaned out of his carriage window to salute two child prodigies of eight and twelve hurrying down a path. 'And although . . . differently dressed . . . the King put his head out, and, laughing, greeted us with head and hands—particularly our Master Wolfgang.' In Salzburg, a portrait of a chubby boy, in a suit of violet brocade with Venetian ruffles and a bejewelled sword and scabbard at his side, recalls the scene. Such had been the gifts of doting foreign royalty—although on this, the Mozarts first visit to London, twenty-four guineas had been their 'only patronage', for a three-hour concert, from the King of England.

A few months later, the child composed a set of sonatas, and his father sat down to the task of a dedication. A printer in the Strand was hired and a title page was designed whose flowery lettering might prove in keeping with the French inscription. A messenger was dispatched, and before the day was over, Her Majesty, in accepting the gracious tribute, responded with a bag of fifty sovereigns.

Years later, long after the composer had died in poverty, these sonatas changed hands at three times the original price. Again, along the Queen's Walk down which the messenger had sped that summer's morning in 1764, properties have as constantly changed hands as their prices have trebled—or their names altered.

---

[1] St. George's Hospital is due to be moved out into the countryside, and in its place a luxury hotel is to be built. This is due to be carried out in the 1960s.

York House, with its rather dull Bath stone elevations embodying a Corinthian order, has had three different addresses within a century. Today it is known as Lancaster House;[1] but in 1912 when the first Viscount Leverhulme gave it to the nation as Stafford House, it had previously belonged to the Sutherland family, the third Duke of whom had been an ardent supporter in the 'Sixties of the Suez Canal scheme.

Along this front too, behind varying façades, Georgian architects re-cast interiors in brilliant mimicry of Oppendordt, Boffrand and Verberckt, so that to the drawing-rooms of the Regency were introduced all the gilt splendours of the *salons* of Louis Quatorze—a taste that still lasted when the Ritz was built (on the site of Walsingham House) in the reign of Edward VII.[2] Or in Spencer House or Bridgewater House, listening to the sighs of the poplars, red-faced diners would let stories slip of Prinny saying to his niece, 'Give me your little paw,' and of the ever-watching eyes of her mother, the Duchess of Kent; then as some of the company drowsed and the wine coaster slid from hand to hand, so another would add how on Tuesday, driving in the Park, he had seen His Majesty pop her Highness and child into his phaeton as they made off for Virginia Water—at which another member, determined not to be outvied, brought in a tale of the last evening and how the child, at being asked what her favourite tune was, had replied: 'God save the King, sir.' Snatched from his reveries, an ambassador would mumble something about the prodigies of nature; a musical genius of eight; and his improvisations at Buckingham House on the bass part of an air by Handel. The reigns of George III and George IV became telescoped as his voice was lost in a discussion of a modern cure for gout, royal physicians, and the expectancy of life. Or along this sweep of houses, where only the death-watch beetle or bombing have opened the way for super blocks of luxury flats, other architects have more recently been called in to convert slip rooms into offices, or to make extra bedrooms on attic floors for country members up for the night. In such Clubs, as old hands fondly

[1] See p. 42 also.

[2] It was designed by Mewes & Davis in 1906. The arcade over the pavement was one of the first steel-framed buildings to appear in London.

caress the crystal neck of the decanter, a glittering of many facets lie within the grasp of memory: perhaps that evening at Stafford House when as the young Queen mounted the stairs, pausing as the rhythm halted, so the curtsies of her guests sank with all the white dazzle of swansdown on each step,[1]—or perhaps those odd interests of the third Duke which included orange groves in Florida, clearing the swamps in Egypt, and the art of preserving sea-food for voyages. (He lent Garibaldi his yacht for the purposes of gun-running.)

Thus it is by such tokens that the past is carried to another generation —and the power of anecdote is always as instructive as it is irresistible. 'My boy, in *our day* we never had latch-keys. What were servants for?' Yet as the *Blitzkreig* made gaps in the Queen's Walk, so post-war, tighter economies have made gaps in social life. The gainers have been both the prospectors and speculators, as into the auction-rooms have come Queen Anne desks, water-colours by Varley or Cox, Regency sofas, and Bèron clocks from the Palais Royal. During the lunch-hour recess, the Queen's Walk has become mainly a dealers' promontory. Mainly, but not entirely. For hope need not die since three centuries ago the same characteristic prevailed—though with this exception: then it was speculative building rather than buying, the sums paid being smaller and the objects bought larger. Today it is that order which has reversed.

Nicholas Hawksmore and William Tufnell[2] were early Eighteenth Century contemporaries; they lived within a few doors of each other and as they strolled in the Park each was accounted a success 'in the eyes of the *Ton*'. Moreover, both were ambitious—Hawksmore socially, Tufnell commercially. The first, a senior civil servant, died the owner of an estate, extensive London property and was styled Esquire at the reading of his will: the second, a former bricklayer, amassed over £30,000, but died without estate, a coat of arms or a carriage. The difference is revealing.

Tufnell respected Hawksmore as his social superior, but it was Tufnell who laid the foundations for that wealthy class whose accrued

---

[1] 'I have come from my house to your palace,' Her Majesty would frequently repeat on arriving.

[2] Not to be confused with Captain Samuel Tuffnell, the architect, who worked, under Labelye, on Westminster Bridge in the same century.

fortunes enabled them to dominate the Victorian era. Hawksmore, the architect-*cum*-artist, had conformed to the *status quo*, whereas Tufnell, the capitalist, had proved himself a social builder as well. This is a curious paradox—one that emotionally disturbs many who eat in the surrounding Clubs that lend this area a male exclusiveness. For it is a paradox that applies to all branches of the arts.

At midday, these Clubs fill with young men whose sensitive features suggest that a little more sticking power and they would have followed the way of the arts, not commerce. Between them and the established business men are the *entrepreneurs*—the literary agents, Third Programme producers and publishers whose trade in the arts so often leads to the dilemma of inflating into the real thing the second-rate simply because it sells, justifies expense accounts, and keeps them well protected behind Queen Anne desks. They lack the decisive action which would have made of them an impresario in either publishing or the theatre, since instead their aim has become solely to play safe, remain financially secure—and yet disguise the fact. In the end it is the dilettante, not the genuine artist, who suffers most at their hands, because it is these dilettantes with their caged sensitivity who are soonest heard acquiescing as parties are planned for the Opera—not so much for the singing as for the gaining of useful contacts. Waiting for a table, whiskies are ordered and doubled; later menus are misread, while only occasionally does a young nephew (with the lost soul of a poet) colour behind his spectacles as the promised *hommard* proves to be homemade pie.[1]

Thackeray thought of 'this part of the world' as 'the mart of news'. Certainly the word 'Apartments' on fanlights still recalls the residential heyday when Sir Isaac Newton and Marlborough lodged in St. James's Street (it used to be nicknamed 'Long Street'), Burke and Alfieri within five minutes of them, and Swift, Steele and Handel within another five. In their journals, diaries or autobiographies, Green Park is frequently mentioned—although it is not until the Nineteenth Century that the suggestion occurs of the Park being formed into a series of terraces falling away to the south. In fact, though Boodle's, Brook's and White's were all founded in the Eighteenth Century, this

[1] On Belgian menus this dish is wisely described as *philosophe*.

107

Park often served as a sort of upper terrace for their members just as today it often serves to whet the appetite for a business luncheon and later as an aid to good digestion and the clinching of a deal. For these Clubs—and many more besides—lie within a few minutes' walk, and as once the rolling hillock drew forth the rapier as well as the sonnet, so now the leafy steeple draws forth speculation so high that the figures gambled assume a mythical reality, and there is a feeling abroad that any afternoon there may be the winning bid which may create another Partridge, Christie or Sotheby. For the Knocking-Time is always Now; in war, or love, or business, snap decisions are a deciding factor. To be bold is to speculate, and on this upper ground, with its suggestion of a shelved platform, military rank, tempestuous passion and amassed fortune have all been hazarded. The historic scenes of Green Park have all been tempered with a note of the histrionic.

For instance, when the land about Pikadilla was scarcely disturbed between one reign and the next—save for the cries of boys or wood pigeons clapping their wings in the dark oaks—the first warlike cannon to shatter the peace came from a battery on Hay Hill. The author of *The Dreadful Dragon* did not know of this when he wrote his famous tale—though may be it is not too fanciful to suppose that the event may have left an imprint on the air. Chronologically, Sir Thomas Wyatt's rebellion postdates the dragon by more than thirty-nine thousand years—though between a writer's fiction and that moment in the 'Fourteen-'Eighteen war when he picked up his pen, who would deny that he may not also have picked up some of the events which occurred on that bleak winter's morning in 1554?[1]

(The perceptive are those that are in tune with their subject; they see more clearly, it is said, because they have vision—and vision of one kind perhaps, however fleeting, is no more than an ability to materialize the past. Science lags behind faith—and yet in the progress of science the natural is constantly helping to explain the supernatural and so close the gap. A television set is a highly complex piece of machinery by which certain waves of the ether are picked up and materialized; but the complexities of its inner workings are nothing compared with

[1] *The Dreadful Dragon* was delayed in publication, not appearing until 1928. But it was written more than a decade earlier.

the complexities of the inner workings of man's mind. Yet even in the vocabulary that is applied to television—'being in tune'; 'fixing the picture'; 'picking up the wavelength'—lies a whole range of experience which man has conquered technically, but whose range transmitted back into terms of his own life still offers immense areas of experience to conquer. For this reason alone perhaps it is difficult to believe that the end of the world is near—although to this parenthesis a return will be made when I come to discuss the house of Samuel Rogers which, before it was destroyed by enemy action, used to look out across the Park.)

So it was that on the 5th February as Wyatt's rebels advanced, word had gone to the Earl of Pembroke who had massed the Queen's men north of the Thames in a line reaching from Charing Cross to Constitution Hill. There they had waited until the enemy had come down Hay Hill and were advancing across the 'drie ditch bankes': when almost the whole column had reached the Mall, Pembroke's men saw Wyatt's tail, 'upon which they did set and cut off'. Such is Stow's description of the tactics; others, perhaps remembering the flash of cannon and the scorched ground, likened the tail to a dragon's. Indeed, in the Spain of that time, while the *Gran Capitan*, Conzalo Fernandez de Cordoba, was having his victories, so St. Theresa was having her visions—visions which become much easier to understand if they are seen against a kaleidoscope of sweating faces and empty ladders rising from a dancing inferno of smoke and flame. For both Hell-fire and dragons were as much bound up with the late mediaeval conceptions of war as both man's inhumanity to man and the notion of Angels at Mons were bound up with the sentiments of those on the home front during 1916. Prevailing conceptions of Heaven and Hell are always coloured by the existing conceptions of war and peace—and *coloured* is the operative word.

The next time that Green Park resounded with the tramp of marching men was under the Puritan occupation; in the northern and southern fields of the capital, earthen forts made sinister cornerstones in the scene. As the grey redoubt and battery built on Constitution Hill weathered, so did the jokes. 'Round-headed cuckolds come dig', began one ditty—although, four years later, the Royalists were spreading a propaganda in which the dun colouring of Puritan existence was being compared with the hard ridges of mud that had formed round these forts. The land had gone into mourning for lack of a sun, was a typical conceit whose ambiguity was such that it might refer to the Son of God, or the late king's exiled son. When Parliament therefore passed a vote 'that the works about London be demolished . . . to ease the charge of maintaining and keeping them', this was more in the nature of an excuse than a reason.

A nation demands highlights in its everyday living; and some form of sovereignty—be it religious, royal, or even republican—is a necessary prerequisite for national contentment. In Soviet Russia, the ballerina is treated as a kind of queen—and in England at the time of a Coronation, Communist feeling will often manifest itself by suggesting that the country's miners should sit with the Peers in Westminster Abbey. Yet whereas in both Moscow and London crowds will sometimes queue all night to see a ballet, no similar response in either country has ever been known to greet a miners' march. Likewise tradition has invested the Peers with a kind of divinity, just as the Russian ballerina is considered as a star—a term that straightaway suggests someone specially apart. So, too, with the film-star. Outside the Ritz, in 1935, when girls ran after the cigarette stubbs that Robert Taylor had thrown in the gutter, there may have been mob hysteria in the tussle to get them, but, in some respects, the act could be paralleled in the fight for relics in other ages. If the pin-up may have taken the place of the saint, then the reason may be that, whereas the photograph still bears a semblance of reality, the statue of repository art has become no more than an unrecognizable neuter in a nightgown; or, if jazz may have taken the place of hymn-singing, then the reason may be that whereas the song-writer has remained lively the hymn-writer has become a mournful dowd.[1] Such swing-overs in taste may be regretted but not denied. After all, the crooner may yet prove to be the modern psalmist in disguise, since those who would argue from such a premise that this is a post-Christian world have failed to realize how essentials like the necessity of worship are so vital a part of man's nature that if their

---

[1] Just before this book went to press, Louis Armstrong said on television: 'Jazz is a universal language—more powerful than any masonry.'

XXXII. A View of the Queen's Walk, Green Park, 1797; an engraving by Storer, after a drawing by E. Dayes.

XXXIII. A perspective View of the Temple of Peace, Green Park, 1749; a contemporary print sold by Robert Wilkinson of Cornhill.

expression is cramped or prevented they are just as capable of breaking out on the dance-floor. Properly understood, in the Bolshoi Theatre or inter-planetary travel lies a symbol of hope for the persecuted Church in Russia, since it testifies unconsciously to the need men have of setting their lives by a star (or stars). The Soviet rulers are careful not to extinguish every light because they know that to do so would be to drain existence of all colour.

For example, to revert to the Puritans, when they closed the play-houses they soon found themselves being flouted—notably in the parks, since it was in the parks that fashion broke out in all its range of colour. Revolting colour, added some of their divines—only to be answered: Yes, a Revolt *of* Colour. The failure of the Levellers was ultimately a failure to reduce everything to one dreary level. Subsequent rulers have always been wise in displaying themselves to their people—and no better display grounds have they found than the parks.

With the reign of Charles II, houses began to flank St. James's Fields, while Picadilly, on its northern side, saw the erection of many classical palaces. Careful tree plantings and a network of gravel paths were laid out in Green Park and St. James's Park. The Great Fire of 1666 burnt away the frontiers of the old City, and by Queen Anne's accession London was no longer two cities but one. Fine red brickwork crept down the avenues and parterres, until with the peace of 1714 and a new Royal House, Hanover Square set a fresh fashion in architecture. By the time of George II, the new brickwork was 'grey', since 'red' was considered 'too hot' to go in combination with stone and white painted wood. (But 'grey' meant usually either a reddish brown or yellow.) In the West End, parapetted rows of houses replaced the tabled streets. St. George's Hospital, set for infection's sake at the edge of the fields, was a private residence, converted by Ware—a feat that was made possible—as in the case of the London, Westminster and Middlesex Hospitals—by the support of a regular body of annual subscribers who were also medical enthusiasts.[1]

On the way between Kensington Palace and Whitehall, George II

---

[1] In this paragraph and some earlier ones I have paraphrased much of what Sir John Summerson has written at length. I acknowledge the debt with pleasure—his books are models of excellence. See Bibliography.

and his Queen would frequently pass it. A sudden bump in the King's New Road would cause him to grunt, reminding him as they approached the Hyde Park turnpike of the patients close by; he would tap his wife's shoulder—though more often than not her mind was dreaming of how she might improve Green Park as she had improved Kensington Gardens. So it was on these carriage rides that she planned the Walk, which later bore witness to her name, and had a pavilion erected, which she called her Library. The latter was set near the ice houses mentioned in Rugge's *Diurnal*, published in the reign of Charles II. But because it was Charles II's reign they are mentioned as being in St. James's Park whereas in actual fact they were in Green Park. 'A snow house and an ice house, made in St. James's Park, as the mode is in some parts of France and Italy and other hot countries, for to cool wines and other drinks for the summer season'[1]. The same faulty geography persists in Waller's poem known as 'St. James's Park'.

> Yonder the harvest of cold months laid up
> Gives a fresh coolness to the royal cup;
> There ice, like crystal firm and never lost,
> Tempers hot July with December's frost.

The ice houses remained until the early Nineteenth Century: but with Queen Caroline's death her Library, where she had breakfasted ten days before she died, was allowed to fall into disrepair. Finally, its shell became a beacon of victory to mark the public celebrations held for the Peace of Aix La Chapelle in 1749. 'An act of vandalism, it must never be repeated,' said the critics. But it was, not once but thrice. . . .

[1] The ice-house mount can still be seen opposite No. 119 Piccadilly.

II

NOW THAT THE War of Succession was over, great preparations were afoot. In Green Park, a Temple of Peace was
to mark the event. Should it be Ionic, Corinthian or Doric—
asked Servandoni, who had built St. Geneviève in Paris, and then,
without pausing for a reply, he answered: 'The Style shall be Doric.'

A skeleton, four hundred and ten feet long and one hundred and
fourteen feet high, was soon standing. Next came the orders for the
carpenters to prepare frets; for the glass-makers to blow lustres; for
the wire-makers to create flowers—and for the painters to let allegory
be their inspiration. Yet these orders came from a sick-bed. Hardly
had they been issued with instructions that a canvas twenty-eight foot
by ten be also painted of His Majesty, attended by Mars and Neptune,
than de Casali had to be called in to supervise the work for Servandoni.
So to the roof, high on a pole, was affixed a sun whose candle power
was intended to turn the Park's night into day. In a rare print of the
time, this sun gives the impression of resembling a monstrance (Plate
XXXIII, facing p. 111); but the novelty of it was sufficient to make
Londoners forgive the possible papist insinuation.

In the centre, surmounted by the Duke of Montagu's arms, was set a
musical gallery. Handel was asked to write a grand military overture.
The music was to be stormy, a sea swelling in anger and then as
suddenly dying into a calm. As there should be allegory in the paintings
of adornment, so there should be allegory in the music chosen: Handel's
theme must be war and peace.

Later, back in 57 Brook Street, the composer's hand reached for a
pencil; phrases crashed like waves in his mind—forty trumpets, twenty
French horns, sixteen hautboys, twelve side drums, eight kettle drums
and, to override all, 'a hundred cannon to go off singly with the music'.
Lord Chesterfield had called musicians the 'fiddlers of the Town', yet
now the Town came begging their services. Every day as the work

progressed solicitous enquiries were made, even by Lord Chesterfield's servants. One morning before breakfast news came that a plank had fallen loose of the scaffolding and hit de Casali. Fortunately, just as Handel was salting his porridge he learnt that the hurt was only a temporary one. As normal, after breakfast, he once more returned to his bachelor's sanctuary trying to recapture the sound of billows. 'Vot are billows?' he had one night knocked up a librettist and, on being informed, had returned to his carriage repeating, 'Oh, de vave, de vave.' In the Park, as the building went apace, so now he tried to conjure the effect of breakers growing heavier while the skies thundered. Sunday could be no day of rest, and as he worked, so Londoners turned out in their hundreds to see their new gorgeous Temple. Soon the hundreds became thousands. Many ladies lost the tails of their gowns and many of their beaux lost part of the gold embroidery of their coats as well as their silver-hilted swords. At last out of the throng, one beau turned to his lady: 'Madam, I perceive you are undragonned.'

On Monday, there was a daylight rehearsal. Some fireworks were let off and a few rockets penetrated as deep as five feet into Constitution Hill. Some casualties were taken to St. George's, and these early disasters spread a general desire to forestall others. It was remembered how, after the 'Forty-Five Rebellion the Duke of Cumberland had victoriously paraded his own Regiment of Light Dragoons north of Buckingham House; their short carabines, slung to their side by a moveable swivel, made them a new type of light cavalry that all were anxious to inspect. Anticipating therefore a large crowd, the gates to the Park were ordered to be shut so that the flow of spectators could be checked. Yet determined not to be marshalled thus, the populace took the law into their own hands by tearing down the railings. For at this time, along the northern and western boundaries, railings were fitted in between the gaps that had been left in the wall. The idea was to provide peeps 'of the beautiful convexity of [the Park's] two gently rising hills'—although cries echoed all through the Eighteenth Century to demolish the brick wall set up by Charles II. To avoid a repetition of the 'Forty-Five celebrations, a fifty-foot breach was made in the Piccadilly wall—just after Easter.

On the morning of the 27th April, the King inspected three regiments of Footguards under the command of the Duke of Cumberland. In the early part of the evening he went to the Queen's Library, while the Prince and Princess of Wales, who were on bad terms with their father, decided to keep aloof and watch the firework display from the home of their friend, the Earl of Middlesex's house in Arlington Street. For the Privy Council, the Peers and the Commons, special stands had been erected; but as there were still some free places invitations were extended to the Mayor, his Aldermen, the Directors of certain City Companies and a few 'very important guests.' Amongst these were Handel, Servandoni (up from his bed) and de Casali—also Tyers, the master of the Vauxhall Pleasure Gardens, who was responsible for the illuminations.

As darkness fell, so the grand overture began. Then, at half-past eight, two rockets were released as a sign that the display was about to begin. The cannon within the *chevaux-de-frise* were fired and a hundred and one guns answered from Constitution Hill. Hardly had the sound died away, than the Temple 'with its ten arcades for cannon' caught alight: there followed a tremendous scramble to rush away the hundreds of pounds of powder stored—and, as the scramble became more hectic—, so two arches were burnt before the firemen's hoses reached the scene. Again, so exciting had proved this distraction that most of the fireworks had gone off unnoticed. But a catalogue of their names and quantities, issued by the Board of Ordnance, may still prove 'acceptable . . . to those interested in matters pyrotechnic.' (What a poem Clough could have made from such a list!):

> 10,650 skyrockets, from 4 oz. to 6 pounds weight,
> 87 air balloons,
> 88 tourbillons,
> 21 regulated pieces,
> 30 figured pieces,
> 180 pots d'aigrettes,
> 12,200 pots de brin,
> 21 cascades,
> 131 vertical suns and wheels,
> 71 fixed suns,
> 160 fountains,
> 260 gerves,
> 2,700 lances,
> 5,000 marrons.

These fireworks were all Italian in origin, being made by Messrs. Ruggieri and Sarti of Bologna, and let off under the direction of 'Ch. Frederick, Esq., Comptroller, and Capt. Thomas Desaguliers, Chief Fire-Master of His Majesty's Laboratory'.

Yet in spite of the careful preparations, there was a long list of casualties. One rocket burst in a stand, severely burning the niece of Sir John Peachy. A boy fell from a tree; a drunken cobbler drowned in the central marsh. Servandoni was taken into custody for drawing a sword on Charles Frederick. In all, £90,000 had been spent. The Queen's Library had been burnt out, while for a few months the Temple remained, growing more derilect every day. Then one morning its absence was noted. Who issued the orders for its final dissolution nobody seemed to know. The grass all around grew again and when the next peace festivities were held not a trace of it remained.

During this century interval, Green Park became a site for duels. Endless lists have been issued, but for the most part they make dull reading. By far and away the most exciting was that between Viscount Ligonier and Count Alfieri, the Italian tragedian and poet.

In his *Vita*, which he published at the age of forty-one, Alfieri divided his life into five sections corresponding to Boyhood; Adolescence; Young Manhood; Manhood; and Old Age. In the last chapter in the 'Epoch of Adolescence', the heading reads: 'My Second and Most Amorous Hold-Up in London'. This occurred in Green Park, about the beginning of the summer in the year 1771.

For some months, Ligonier's wife had been Alfieri's mistress.

I had already . . . at great risk to us both been introduced into her own house by her own self—to which the smallness of the London house lent itself, as well as the doors being kept shut and the servants for the most part in the basement. These conditions leave it possible for a person who is on the inside of the street door to open it and easily introduce somebody from the outside into a room on the ground floor which immediately adjoins the door. Consequently, my clandestine admissions were all thoroughly successful. . . .

(It is curious that such dramatic architecture, so useful in the construction of a play of intrigue, should have been so little used by English dramatists.) Anyway, as Alfieri's affair prospered, he grew bolder;

XXXIV. 'Two Impures of the *Ton* off to a Gigg Shop'; a cartoon by R. Dighton, printed by Sayer & Bennet.

XXXV. The Temple of Concord, Green Park, 1814; an engraving by Sands, after a drawing by J. P. Neale.

passion quadrupled his courage and he even pursued his mistress to her country house, where he would visit her after dark. Yet as he grew bolder, so her husband began to grow suspicious: he paid spies to watch her, and at length rewarded with proof, name and time, he left for Town in pursuit of the foreigner. At the Opera, he found him in the meantime, Alfieri had scented danger and hearing a tap on the door of the box, he excused himself to his host and hostess, the Spanish Ambassador and his wife. Quickly he led the way to the foyer where a brief exchange of words followed.

'Here I am,' I cried. 'Who wants me?'

'I do. I want you because I have something to say to you. Let us go outside.'

I replied, 'I am at your service.'

So without further ado, they both left the Haymarket Theatre and 'proceeded, a fairly long distance [mounting passion doubtless elongated the distance], to St. James Park where a gate leads into a large meadow which is called "Green Park" '. As was customary with the evening dress of the period, they both carried swords and while Alfieri was unsheathing his, Ligonier noticed that he had his left arm in a sling and had 'the generosity to ask whether this would prevent [him] from fighting'. His opponent thanked him, said that it would not and immediately began to thrust. 'I have always been a bad fencer . . . and like one in despair, regardless of all the rules of the art . . . , all I sought was to get myself killed.' So despite the broken clavicle of two days before, he charged like a bull; and the simile is in context because the setting sun behind his enemy was like a red rag—it prevented him from seeing as much as it drew him on.

After eight minutes, Alfieri received a wound in the arm, 'neither so deep as a well, nor so large as a church door', and Ligonier seeing his opponent bleeding, put up his sword and, satisfied that his honour had been avenged, strode proudly away. Twenty years later the poet summed up: 'My view is that he did not kill me because he did not want to, and I did not kill him because I did not know how.'

Yet at the time, Count Vittorio Alfieri, bent upon not allowing Viscount Ligonier's proud gesture to pass unrivalled, returned to the Haymarket and sat through the last act. As he re-entered the box he whispered to his host and hostess that he had suddenly remembered urgent business and that it was this that had accounted for his peremptory exit. After the performance, so swiftly had the news of the duel travelled, that when fortune guided him 'to the house of the wronged husband's sister-in-law' who should he meet there to bathe his hurts but his faithful mistress.

A divorce followed—a particularly seamy one because while on one hand the Viscount was claiming heavy damages so the Count on the other learnt that his greatest rival had not been the husband, but one of the grooms. For the occasion, the milliners designed a bonnet known as *le coquine*, which rendered a fan unnecessary.

With the Whigs in full command of Taste, the 'Seventies was a high period for duelling. As fast as the fires of love fanned a quarrel, so fast went honour to the stake. The laws of social behaviour demanded that if a man was challenged he must answer with his sword. Illicit relationships were accepted provided that they were maintained discreetly; but society would not stand for them being vulgarly flaunted. In breaking this rule, the Duke of Grafton had laid himself open to censure; by obeying them, Count Alfieri had kept the names of his amours from the scribblers. Only the divorce, in which by unlucky chance he had been involved, focussed their attention on him. For the fact that Viscountess Ligonier had let her passions run with her to a groom in the stable was not accounted shocking because she had already provided a male heir and her own promiscuity was her own affair. Mrs. Sheridan, too, was more alarmed that her husband had let himself be caught in a ludicrous rather than a compromising position—though for the woman in question she cared not a rap either way. 'I was afraid I was going to have the gout the other day. I believe I live too chaste', wrote a Peer—and then sighed: 'It is a common fault with me.' So far the inhibitions of a contraceptive mentality had not appeared. A child might be delivered safely in France or Italy, or it might be born secretly and cast into the Serpentine, or occasionally one would be drowned in the pool that lay in the middle of Green Park. Illegitimacy was no stigma to social success. Lady Yarmouth received two legacies from two gentlemen who both claimed they were her father. Nor did she complain; she simply revelled in the knowledge that now she was twice as rich.

Duelling meant that there could be blood-letting, and the parks were ideal meeting-grounds; feuds and killings were experiences not vicariously enjoyed in the cinema, but as part of the Town's life. The clash of swords, or exchange of fire, made a religion of honour and honour in turn became the religion of tragedy. Robert Wilberforce was particularly worried by this axiom; he remembered how Christ had told St. Peter to put up his sword and he began to realize that the laws of honour were not necessarily the same as those of the Church. He became tormented with the obsession that were he challenged he might be either forced to disobey his conscience, or else be dubbed a coward and so lose social caste. Already, so he learnt, the Church of Rome had placed Alfieri's autobiography on the Index, while Horne Tooke, his contemporary, artfully announced that he would never fight a duel in any park, thus rendering it impossible for anyone to insult him without incurring a charge of cowardice since they knew that he could not fight back.

To laugh *with* Horne Tooke is as easy as it is to laugh *at* Wilberforce. After all, duelling is not a problem of this age. Yet the dilemmas of human frailty do not alter, only the social stresses change. In the modern craze for witch-hunts in politics and morals, where shall a man's loyalty lie—to his friends or his country? This is not a hypothetical problem, but a problem quite as real as Wilberforce's dilemma about 'Duelling, Honour and Christian Morality'. In a century's turning, solely the terms of reference have altered: no longer there exists a clear-cut choice between Eighteenth Century honour or Nineteenth Century morality, but frequently, against a more complex background, a choice exists between choosing to be either a liar or an informer. 'Dishonesty or insanity? What use is honesty to an insane mind? Which of us would not choose dishonesty?' So wrote an author of twenty-four, in possibly one of the most publicized enquiries of the 1950s.[1]

Undoubtedly the transition from an Eighteenth Century code of honour to a Nineteenth Century code of morality was gradual (this is a generalization). Again, self-righteousness, hypocrisy and smugness—the cost of excessive Victorian zeal (another generalization) —came as a late aftermath and were not as universal as is sometimes

[1] Colin Wilson in *The Outsider* (1956).

supposed. Moreover, perhaps a hundred years hence they may even appear less so, since historical judgments (and generalizations) must always be undergoing the modifying process of re-orientation; but at the moment, at this stage of the present century, 'a schizoid society' best sums up the latter part of George III's reign.

In 1780, a Sergeant Sparrow of the First Regiment of Footguards robbed a gentleman on Constitution Hill of his watch, chain, and several guineas. Subsequently he was caught, condemned to death, and clapped into Newgate. 'But he was not born to be hanged', wrote Horace Walpole to the Countess of Ossary, 'for he was one of the three hundred criminals set free by the burning of Newgate at the Gordon Riots . . . and was shot as he was spiriting up the rioters.' Walpole, however, had been misinformed. For the same sergeant did escape only to be challenged as a deserter at Barnet by the Hertfordshire Militia. Confessing then that he was an escaped prisoner, he was taken to Hereford Jail and in due course hanged at Tyburn. Such an irony calls forth from Larwood this ludicrous adaptation from *Hamlet*: 'There is a special kind of providence even in the fall of *Sparrow*.'

Exactly a century divides this comment from Walpole's—a century which saw the successful bowdlerization of Shakespeare. In future, fathers reading aloud or actors on the stage must substitute the word 'person' for 'body' and 'corpse'—although Hamlet's, 'I'll go lug the guts into the neighbour room', was permitted to stand as 'body'. Scarcely could Polonius's corpse be described as 'a person'. As always, Larwood's desire was to force a moral judgment—and how far that judgment could be strained is well illustrated in his epitaph for Sergeant Sparrow.

Hannah More began her life as a dramatist, and her friendship with Garrick lasted long after she had vowed never again to enter a theatre. For so severely did her Christianity afflict her that she could not abide the inherent blasphemy in an Oxford College being called, 'All Souls', or a London thoroughfare, 'Trinity Lane'. Such headlines as 'The Salvation of a Nation', 'The Christening of a Ship', or 'The Ascension of a Balloon' distressed her so much that she could not read the paragraphs beneath. When Green Park, therefore, turned from a field of duelling into an ideal ground for balloon ascents, she was equally shocked (Plates XXXVIII and XXXIX, facing pp. 128 and 129). These balloons were an infringement on the divine, man was not made to fly, and it was vainglory that he should attempt to do so. In 1802 when a celebrated French aeronaut successfully landed a cat from a high tower, she did not appreciate the ballad, 'Puss in a Parachute', with its chorus line:

'Twas beginning to rain cats and dogs.

Such feats she accounted among the new follies of the new century, forgetting how once she had sat in bay windows watching the world saunter down the Queen's Walk—an honour for which the owners of these rooms in 1785 had paid anything from £400 (Mr. Hastings) to £4,000 (Mr. Rigby).

Pimlico did not exist, and from these windows on a clear day the countryside could be seen with its pastures and meadows, cut by brooks, rivulets and pools. The wind would whisper over the reeds and rushes, rippling small ponds—while in the distance, a sail bellying out would trace the course of the lost Thames through the chequered fields of the City's outskirts. Inevitably the water colours of this panorama became influenced by the Dutch masters. In fact, it was the converting of these pools, rivulets and brooks by the Water Companies, such as that of Chelsea, that led to the reservoir system, such as existed in the north-east corner of Green Park which until 1855 held 1,500,000 gallons. (Here, Benjamin Franklin showed the experiment of smoothing waves by pouring oil on them). Indeed, to think of this landscape is to forget the windows of Messrs. Hastings and Rigby (who were they?) and remember instead the magnificent views of the Park from Devonshire House or No. 22 St. James's Place, the home of Samuel Rogers.[1] Not that Hannah More ever entered either—though in one her influence was profoundly felt, in the other widely discussed.

Devonshire House, built in the preceding reign, was the crowning

[1] Or to come up to comparatively recent times there is Sylvia Lynd's telling description of Hugh Walpole's home at No. 90 Piccadilly. '. . . T'ang horses stepping grandly on the chimney-piece; the white Utrillo, a new possession, propped on the arms of an armchair; all sorts of trifles in jade and rose-quartz and amber giving back the light; the window filled with his big Epstein bronzes, the Green Park for their background. . . .' *The Book Society News*, July 1941.

glory of Whig grandeur. The Duchess's father was one of the richest commoners in England; and, as frequently happened, he lived to see both his daughters marry early into the aristocracy.[1] (Hannah More had infiltrated from the middle classes to the upper; entry was open to wealth and talent—and, an early widow, she had both money of her own and was already the author of several works when she first reached London.) So at eighteen, Georgiana, Duchess of Devonshire, secure in her new home, listened to gavottes on the clavichord, skimmed through *Les Liaisons Dangereuses,* and cultivated the cooing accent which became known as 'the Devonshire drawl'. In a secluded boudoir, she would sit before the fire with an uncut version of Shakespeare—dreaming idly of the heart's affections; the smile that speaks more than a sonnet; and the piercing tenderness of lips that burn all save their presence away. She thought she died because she could not die; she was Venus and Héloise made flesh in the paint of Gainsborough. Love was the key to her life and love alone could offer itself; those who sought to gain anything else, did not deem themselves worthy to experience it. This love covered Georgiana's existence in a net more difficult to break than any wrought by Vulcan; the texture of the meshes was so closely knit that she could not escape. She had provided her husband with a male line with their third child and, not forgetting the stories told of Viscountess Ligonier, she was prepared in her quest as a sensualist to mount to whoever should hold the stirrup. Under her own roof, she accepted with well-mannered grace a *menage à trois,* while the noise of children filled the nurseries on the upper floors at a surprising speed. After all, the Duke's children by Lady Elizabeth Foster could not be left in France once Revolution had broken out. Fox and Sheridan were frequent vistors and so was the Prince of Wales; to the routs, balls, and fitful analyses of emotion by the hour were added gambling and dissipations of every kind. Pitt had fallen from power in 1784 and without the restraint of parliamentary office, speculation at the card tables became ever higher; and at cards, as in love, they played with panache and good temper; if they lost, they lost as gentlemen. Wilberforce could not but deplore Fox's insatiable taste for gambling— and yet he loved the man for 'his frank and friendly temper'.

[1] His other daughter became Lady Bessborough.

With Georgiana's death everything changed. Her younger sister by two years, Harriet, now left to live alone at Devonshire House, would not countenance her father's liaison with Lady Elizabeth and lived in a perpetual fear lest on a trip to Brighton she might be forced to curtsey to the Prince of Wales with his mistress. After her husband's death, like Hannah More, she devoted herself to philanthropic deeds. This *volte-face* was the work of Selina Trimmer.

Selina Trimmer, a governess who had fallen under the sway of Hannah More's ideas, had been sent to Devonshire House by her mother in something of the way in which a missionary might be primed before being sent into a foreign land. Certainly her teachings were not without effect. Harriet was one convert to her credit. Yet to remember Harriet's stepsister, Caroline Lamb, is to be put in mind of the schizoid nature of the household. For the difference between sister and stepsister was not so much a personal antagonism as a dividing of the ways: Caroline was following a lone star, whereas Harriet was following the main trend. Within three reigns the complete character of Devonshire House had been altered, because as Victoria's reign approached so a certain flatness crept into its social life; the ice of His Grace's champagne now affected the ice of Her Grace's manner. In a word, everywhere the Season was becoming respectable. When a rhymster like Winthrop Mackworth Praed writes, 'A Goodnight to the Season', he must needs cap his verses with a moral from *Hamlet*: 'So runs the world away.'

As the artist's position in the Eighteenth Century had resembled that of a lackey—a writer cowering in ante-rooms for subscriptions while musicians, roped off in the drawing-room, awaited the guineas of their betters—, so by Victorian times the artist gradually came to be thought of as a fully-fledged rebel; and pretty generally that title holds (the terms 'outsider' and 'bounder' have been more recently added). Yet once an artist is successful, invitations pour upon him from social hostesses, organizing committees of Charity, and he begins to be lack-eyed in the Clubs by all those who have their eye on subsidiary ex-ploitation by means of film, radio or television adaptations. The *entrepreneurs* are quick with their lionizing hospitality—and so they have ever been, it is asserted, as soon as the name of Samuel Rogers crops up. But this is a detraction. With his private means, Rogers could so easily have been either an editor or publisher, art dealer or reviewer if he had wished; instead he realized that his true talents lay elsewhere and preferred to make himself the impresario of the breakfast-table. And never had breakfast parties become such legends as his.

Next to Spencer House stood No. 22, built by James Wyatt, and his London home from 1808-1855 (Plate XXXVII, facing p. 125). In that year, in an obituary, a Mr. Miller wrote: 'The name of Samuel Rogers alone saves Green Park from oblivion, and gives it a popularity which but for him it would never possess.' The same obituary also said:

Within [his] house, every distinguished literary man of the last century had been a guest. Here Scott, Byron, Shelley, Coleridge and Campbell have many a time discoursed. . . . What a rich volume that would be, were it possible to write it, that contained all the good sayings that have been uttered beneath that roof! Here I first sat as a guest, roaring with laughter at the wit of Sydney Smith; here also I have listened 'with bated breath' to the music murmured by the lips of Tommy Moore. Within those walls I first saw the true poetess and much injured lady, Caroline Norton, and from the host himself in my early career as an author received that kindness and encouragement without which I might have 'fallen by the way'. A description of this celebrated house, of all it contains, and of all the guests it has received, would require the hand of another Horace Walpole to illustrate it.

But this is to begin at the wrong end. . . .

Before 1808, Rogers had published two slim volumes of poetry. As a young man he had called on Dr. Johnson in Bolt Court, pulled the bell, and then run away in shyness. (Alan Pryce-Jones, lately Editor of *The Times Literary Supplement*, tells a similar story of his first meeting with Raymond Mortimer—although in this case his courage stuck and he waited for the door to be opened.) At table-talk, Rogers' chief merit was not so much repartee—which he could use stingingly enough—, but the gift of the born raconteur. His memory stretched back to when Mrs. Thrale, the widow of a wealthy brewer, had become Mrs. Piozzi, the wife of a singing master, and he would mimic Dr. Johnson and Lord Chesterfield in their rage as both had thundered against such a marriage of beer and song. Again, the peace celebrations of 1814 and the proposed Temple of Concord reminded him of the 1749 Temple of Peace—even if at one remove: the sites chosen were

XXXVI. 'A Four in Hand in Green Park'; from a painting by J. Pollard, 1819.

XXXVII. Samuel Rogers' House overlooking the Queen's Walk; an engraving by
Duvercier from a Nineteenth Century drawing initialled W.P.

identical, and he could recall how his father had ranted for years about the vandalism, extravagance and waste of £90,000 which it had cost the country. Yet as the new structure went up, he himself felt more temperate: there were so many books to read—and how grateful he was not to be a reviewer! Hannah More's *Coelebs in Search of a Wife* had been out five years, and even so the craze to make clergymen not more dutiful but more respected had not died. But Coelebs, to him, seemed nothing less than a dummy. With his long sight, Rogers' eye constantly wandered from the page to beyond the palings where a cordon of sentries stood watching the Temple rise. Would that the Evangelical movement might turn into a Classical movement, he must have sometimes wished, for really he could not understand this Mrs. More; she had said that she would derive better satisfaction from lowering the price of bread than writing the *Iliad*. Even now the very thought made him irate. A walk would cure all—and off he would go in the direction of the sentries on guard.

Within a few weeks, the Temple of Concord lay folded away in a Gothic castle of canvas. From its southernmost towers sprang a bridge leading to the roof of Buckingham Guard House. This enclosure intended for the Royal Family was decorated in red, white and blue bunting, while along a temporary ballustrade were set the words in letters as fat as Falstaff:

FIRST OF AUGUST—
PEACE CENTENARY OF THE
ILLUSTRIOUS HOUSE OF BRUNSWICK.

It was anticipated that the Royal Family should parade along this bridge, thus lending Brunswick splendour to the glorious naval names placarded on its edge—Nelson; Strachan; St. Vincent; Brooke; Duncan; Saumarez; Collingwood; Howe. At least, such were the plans. . . .

At six o'clock on the appointed day, the sign that festivities were soon to begin was given by a balloon ascent made by a Mr. Sadler. Yet as he slowly sailed away across the Thames, the people grew restive at the idea of another three hours wait to the fireworks. Many had spent the afternoon trying to conjecture what lay behind the Gothic battlements, while those who said that they believed it was a

Temple were thanked for their pains by being shouted down as nosey-parkers, liars or busybodies. Others who swore that they had seen strips of canvas being fitted over portraits of the Prince Regent and the Bourbons were told that they were spoil-sports; that they must be patient; that in another two hours everything would be revealed.

Those two hours died slowly: but at nine, true to plan, the illuminations were lit—followed by a prolonged cheer. An hour later, an ear-breaking discharge of guns served as a prologue to the promised rocket display. (Sir William Congreve, of rocket fame, was in charge of the whole entertainment.) As gashes of purple and vermilion spray shot upwards filling the sky, so screens fell away and flying buttresses were transformed into Doric columns. As the castle became a Temple (Plate XXXV, facing p. 117), so yellow lamps fringed with red and blue were lit to suggest a building on fire—for it was only by passing through fire that a nation could achieve the strength necessary to live in concord. Those, therefore, who had anticipated these stage effects were now hailed as jolly good fellows; those who had spoken of the portraits of the Prince Regent and Bourbons were now borne shoulder-high as prophets. But as suddenly as the rejoicing had begun, so it ceased; as the dead ash of the rockets floated down, it became remembered that so far neither the Prince Regent nor any member of his family had appeared. Some shouted—yet in vain; others grew angry —yet again without effect. The Prince was snoozing between 'a splendid dinner' and the promise of 'a sumptuous supper'. Fortunately, before the crowd could become unruly, the pagoda in St. James's Park had caught alight and vast numbers were able to forget their royal disappointment in the excitement of shouting instructions to those trying to stop the flames from spreading.[1]

Not until the next morning was the Prince told of its destruction; and not until nearly lunch-time did he go and see what a blackened skeleton had become of the Temple put up to celebrate the centenary of the House of Brunswick.

From the house of Rogers, the day after, there had been a constant procession to the windows to look out across the desolate and charred landscape. At the breakfast table there had been comments—caustic

---

[1] See pp. 182 et seq. for the full story of Nash's pagoda and its fire.

and sardonic, anarchic and democratic—about the value of peace celebrations. However, all these had been silenced as the host had passed a newspaper from hand to hand. The paragraph to which all were directed appeared in the form of an advertisement:

LOST, on Monday night, the beautiful Green Park, which used to extend from St. James' Park to Piccadilly. It is supposed to have been removed by a Mr. John Bull, who was seen here last night with a pretty numerous party, and who has left a brown Park in exchange, of no value, to the Ranger. Information will be received by the two stags over the lodge in Piccadilly.[1]

As the coffee grew cool, so the conversation turned from a discussion of the use and abuse of public holidays to a consideration of the strength of irony—or as a young literary dog out to create a dash put it, 'the iron of irony'. Then once more the conversation pivoted in another direction—this time towards a consideration of the use and misuse of words.

Within a fortnight there occurred the Prince Regent's birthday. The breach in the wall begun in 1749 had recently been widened so that it had now become impossible to limit the numbers entering the Park. On the 14th August, the rumour spread that the skeleton was to rise, clothed in a new array; as the crowds began to gather, so they waited for a miracle; somewhere in the blackness, they believed, lurked a troop of fire-masters ready to release rockets and tourbillons by the score. When none burst in the sky, they attacked the guards and, overpowering them at the odds of a thousand-to-one, they broke inside the enclosure. There they kindled a fire, feeding it at first with twigs and branches, later with palings and sentry-boxes. So high did the sparks leap, that one City fire brigade turned out, believing St. James's Palace to be ablaze. Yet the next day, more satanic than ever, the Temple was still standing.

At Rogers' breakfast table as the daily *Sun* was passed from hand to hand, so eyes in vain skimmed the advertisement columns for the announcement that would declare that 'a brown Park had been lost' and a black one found. By the time the dishes were cleared, the company had fallen to a comparison of the last night's activities with

[1] These stags were subsequently placed over the Albert Gate, Hyde Park, when the Ranger's Lodge was pulled down in the middle 1840s. See p. 71.

those of the Goths. Their host stopped them, recalling how his father had used almost the same words when describing the burning of the Temple of Peace as 'an unparalleled deed of vandalism'. There followed a debate on the nature of barbarism and the repetitions of history. Coming in at one angle, a guest mentioned St. Agatha of the Goths, the parish of St. Alphonsus Liguori, the saint who without leaving his church had yet been present at the funeral of Clement XIV . . . and as they waited for a conclusion, so another guest cut in with the story of Biela's comet, 'that fiery wanderer', which seven years before had drawn as many to Green Park and their telescopes as to their knees and prayers. . . . Neither story was finished, for with a gentle twist Rogers turned both towards a general discourse on astral projection. The climate at No. 22 was noticeably liberal, and with the talent of the perfect impresario, the host saw that his visitors never gave less than their best, guiding rather than domineering their conversation.

A few biographers have sniped spitefully: 'There was not a trace of bonhomie about [him],' stated one of them, William Jerdan. Yet to accept this judgment is to entirely misunderstand the kind of man that he was. If his breakfasts were world famous, then inevitably with the guests slipped in a number of hangers-on. The hanger-on of that period was like the modern gate-crasher. He preyed on human frailty since, however sure a man might be of himself and his appointed place in the literary stratum, there were bound to be moments of doubt when his eye would be fixed less sharply on the door. This is the perpetual price of hospitality because there are always a handful who will abuse it—an abuse which amounts really to a form of jealousy and goes far in explaining the spite of the Jerdans of this world. Again, some of Rogers' protégés who subsequently became eminent, then turned against their guide and critic. Likewise, this was a case of biting the hand that feeds. Ultimately it is the celebrated names of the majority of his guests which has more than insured his future against his detractors. Many besides the Rev. A. A. Coxe, an American minister, must have wished that his walls could have 'boswellized all the *memoribilla* which they heard'—although in some cases it seems as if they did.

One day Wordsworth (who had crossed the Park with Haydon) remarked that the painter was downstairs looking at the collection of

XXXVIII. The Destruction of the Victoria and Albert Balloon above Green Park, 1851; a print issued by Ackermann & Co. a month after the event.

XXXIX. Ballooning above Green Park in the 1850's; a cartoon by John Leech.

Rembrandts, Tintorettos and Reynolds. 'Ah!' murmured his host, 'he is better employed than chattering nonsense upstairs.' After lunch as the painter and poet recrossed the Park, there followed a conversation whose authenticity I cannot trace, but which begins to appear in books of literary gossip about the year 1843. This is how it goes:

Haydon said: 'Scott, Wilkie, Keats, Hazlitt, Beaumont, Jackson, Charles Lamb are all gone—we are only left. How old are you?'
   'Seventy-three, in my seventy-third year; I was born in 1770.'
   'And I in 1786,' said the painter.
   'You have many years before you.'
   'I trust I have; and you, too, I hope. Let us cut out Titian who was ninety-nine.'
   'Was he ninety-nine?' asked the poet.
   'Yes,' replied his friend, 'and his death was a moral; for as he lay dying of the plague, he was plundered, and could not help himself.'

It seems that if the proverb that fits the first part of the story of Rogers, Wordsworth and Haydon was that walls have ears, then it is John Heywood's Sixteenth Century version that fits Wordsworth's and Haydon's afternoon walk: 'Fields have eyes and woods have ears.' The variation is in keeping with the forest alive with listening birds beneath whose branches the two must have made their way back to Paddington that spring afternoon in 1843. For it was this year that 'the melancholy, stagnant pool' had been filled in by order of Lord Ducannon, Chief Commissioner of Forests, and it was in the same spring that the Green Park boundaries had just been increased by the addition of the gardens attached to the Ranger's Lodge. The Ranger's Lodge itself was pulled down shortly after; its enormity of balcony 'made it look like the outrigger of an Indian canoe' and so topheavy did it appear that on Guy Fawkes night, 1835, Londoners had sung that one push was enough to turn it over.

On the more scarred lawns to the south, which marked the sites of the Temples of Peace and Concord, Lord Ducannon had the ground re-turfed. In her later years, Hannah More had devoutly wished that this might be done for the general health of the populace; when instead news was brought to her how one day the area had been roped off as an aeronaut had made a balloon ascent on a horse—both he and his mount staying up for an hour and a half—, it seemed for one delirious moment as if her life 'had availéd nought'.

'The face of the Park was changing.' It is a recurring phrase. In 1817, 'the dinner hour of four and five among the great of the world, having shifted to the unhealthy hour of eight and nine, the promenade in dinner full dress was consequently lost', observed Sir Richard Phillips. No longer at the fountain by the 'romantic shore' of the 'melancholy pool' did hands assume all the liquescence and overflowing of inexhaustible sentiment; gone were the billowing tulle dresses, the sparkling tiaras, and the harlequin variety of uniforms and decorations when early one Season the Duke of Wellington's sister-in-law had eloped across the fields with Lord Paget, so that it was not until dawn that the coachmen at the northern Park gates learnt that they must return home to inform Sir Henry Wellesley of his loss. Yet the failure to re-terrace as well as re-turf the Park lost London a gardens such as those which surround the Giardino Reale in Naples or the Villa Borghese,[1] bewailed the Prime Minister, Sir Robert Peel. In his mind, he had envisaged Roman fountains, statues of the gods, Grecian urns brimming with flowers and balustrades edging each level of the Park as it sloped away to Buckingham Palace; he imagined the Queen's Walk as a slow falling stairway, eased out with frequent balconies. Instead, all he lived to see was 'the miserable fountain drowned in its own stinking lake' (Plate XXXII, facing p. 110), and only once, he claimed, had there been a worthy floral display—in 1809, in the adjoining gardens of Spencer House. Another Prime Minister, Lord Palmerston, noticed that iron hurdles had been set up close to the paths and rebuked the Minister responsible with these words: 'They are an intolerable nuisance, since the purpose of the grass is to be walked on freely and without restraint by the people, old and young, for whose enjoyments the parks are maintained.' So again the face of the Park was changing—and as the term comes to be used nearer to the present so the phrase comes to include not only those who walk beneath its trees but all those who are responsible for pollarding them, sweeping the paths clear of leaves or building those small sad bonfires whose smoke rises so wispily each autumn.

[1] See second part of footnote on p. 94.

III

IN THE FAINT early dawn of one day, 'in the midst of golden summer, a column of smoke was seen rising . . .'. 'Danger to the lives of the dressmakers in Dover Street was not apprehended. The fire brigade had not been called out,' continued Sir Max Beerbohm in his tale of the *Dreadful Dragon of Hay Hill*, 'because the fire brigade had not been called into existence. Dover Street had not been built.' This all happened more than thirty-nine thousand years before the birth of Christ.

If the fallacy still pervades in dozens of guide books of treating Green Park as an Upper St. James's Park, then those who read a paragraph here, notice a newspaper reference or a casual comment in either a journal or novel, must begin to be struck by the strange effects of coincidence in the history of Green Park. For instance, three times in the 1840s an attempt was made to assassinate Queen Victoria driving up Constitution Hill (in the 1930s another attempt was also made on the life of Edward VIII). Again, three times have victory celebrations caused a London crowd to behave more wildly in its precincts than any other royal park. I have told the story of the Temple of Peace, the Temple of Concord, and all the time I have found it difficult to suppress a more recent story—the story of the victory nights after the second World War. For on those nights, London became pandemonium let loose; between the Ritz and St. George's the railings were down (they had been used to make tanks), and a crowd which one minute was tossing naked girls in blankets in Leicester Square, was the next building beacons out of Park chairs.

Naturally on the following day there were the usual Mrs. Grundy headlines, some leader-writers likening the scene to an invasion of Goths and Vandals, just as on two other occasions the words vandalism and Goths had been bandied by other reporters in the same context during the Eighteenth and Nineteenth Centuries. Was this coincidence, or was it that certain deeds fit a certain landscape and become infectious? Or was it that the past leaves its trace in the air, creating a pattern for the assassin or ring-leader of a mob just as an author finds a pattern in his facts and the history which he must tell?

Perhaps at this moment in some Club there is an author discussing this very idea with a publisher, just as a century ago a young man might have come shyly to the breakfast-table of Samuel Rogers. And it may be as he strolls after lunch past No. 22, so his eye will wander over the broken wall covered in falling leaves to the cracked basement floor through which ragwort and fleabane are springing; here, after three hundred years, the seed is burgeoning beneath the stone. In the shifting light between tea-time and dusk, sometimes an ant upon a single grain of corn, willowy and yellow, will mark the division. After I was demobilized I remember cutting from the Park into St. James's Place along this bomb site, watching the fingers of a fern gradually cradle a tin that had been thrown there. At first, wedged against a broken column, the familiar picture of fresh garden peas was brightly stamped on the paper band. Each morning it was the same; but unseen each night the tin grew away from the stone. Then one day it toppled down, washed free of its artificial promises . . .

This could be the material for a prose-poem—the kind of contribution to find its way into a 'little review'; and sometimes it is such parables, beneath vast slabs of Corinthian pilaster, that fall from the lips of young men as they relax their executive masks and once more uncage that sensitivity which an uncle had suppressed more than a decade ago in the same coffee room. For by a strange paradox the Great Clubs have ceased to be the homes of the Great Reviews; 'little reviews' have taken their place, with editorial addresses ranging from bed-sitting-rooms in Bayswater to miners' shacks near Durham. The Clubs have deteriorated, say both the old member and the younger literary historian; but by deterioration they do not mean the same thing. To the literary historian, the Club has declined as a centre of ideas; to the octogenarian, it has declined as a social centre. 'My boy, *these days* they accept anybody—doctors, solicitors, vets.' Such are the voices of the diehard core who would agree with Jacob Larwood when he protested at Beau Brummel being copied by any Mr. Higgins who hailed from regions east of Terra Incognita; and by regions east of Terra Incognita, he meant Temple Bar or Bishopsgate. Or there are those who would still applaud his sentiments in his distaste that Mademoiselle Papillotte from Cranbourne Alley should be allowed to breathe the 'same oxygen as those ladies with blue blood from Grosvenor Square'. His lament that in 1860 Green Park had passed into the undisputed possession of the nursery-maids of neighbouring tradesmen is a familiar refrain—a case of everything deteriorating, standards slipping away, the world crumbling; it is the dirge that is repeatedly being sung. When social critics take it up, it is because the destructive element is easier to advance than the constructive. Blame-the-Present is as useful a scapegoat as Blame-All. In fact, what was happening (and still is happening) is that standards were not slipping but changing, and as they did so, so 'the face of the Park was changing.'

An air of speculation and impermanence lies over Green Park. Gone are the bevies of nursery-maids that once as eagerly watched the escort of Highlanders as they canvassed the growing patch of violet in the Queen's bonnet; today, mews flats in Brick Street and Shepherd Market attract rents as high as the suites of rooms which Mr. Rigby and Mr. Hastings hired at the end of the Eighteenth Century. The Knocking-Time is still Now. Along the Queen's Walk, on a May day, the connoisseur snatches a quick breather and feels himself lucky to be born under Gemini; in the afternoon's bidding he will take a chance on Item 47 being a Tintoretto. An author talks to one of H. G. Wells's old publishers, letting the sun intoxicate his ideas, as he suggests a study on the need for spacemen or angels. As hotel blinds are pulled down, a street walker bows nine times to a pale moon; she turns the money over in her purse and hopes that it may be doubled. Here Wyatt gambled on rebellion in one century, and Handel on a musical cannonade in another. This way a messenger cut from a printer in the Strand with the sonatas of a boy prodigy; this way a runner returned to his dealer with news that these sonatas had been offered in an auction-room. Speculation fills the air with impermanence. Every morning is alive with possibilities; gambles, promoted by premonitions, only wait to be materialized. For every soldier that took a risk one cold February morning, a million lay abed; these hazarded their lives and lost. For every aeronaut that risked a balloon ascent, ten thousand watched earth-bound: these hazarded their lives and were triumphant. For every speculator, there must always be thousands who dare nothing—the thousands to whom Green Park is nothing save a triangle of land, a back way into their offices, or a quick cut to the ministries which surround St. James's Park.

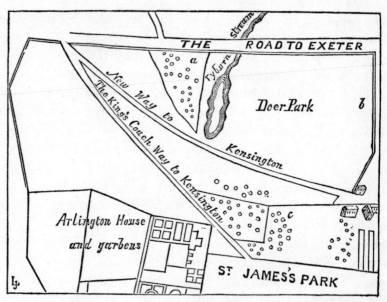

A MAP OF GREEN PARK IN 1696, RECONSTRUCTED BY JACOB LARWOOD, 1881.
a. Enclosure of Ranger's lodge.   *b.* Here the 'Queen's Library' was erected subsequently.   *c.* Wilderness.

PART IV

ST. JAMES'S PARK

ST. JAMES'S PARK

I

ONCE UPON A TIME as the sun set, so the domes, towers and turrets of the City would grow inky; to the south, beyond the fretted cross at Charing, stood the square fortress of the Tower; ahead, lay St. Paul's. Every tree in St. James's was tipped with frost; the winter of 1601 had been bleak, and the days bred a savage blackness. In the heavy panelled rooms of Whitehall, thin wasting fingers retained their sickly strength to curl around the golden orb or sceptre. Every noise affrighted their Queen—the bark of deer; the cough of a serving-man; the sound of cannon in the Estuary. Would ever the Channel be free from invasion? Now the river ran slowly with ice floes; Rosamond's Pond was frozen over. The rookery in the Park seemed sinister and foreboding. Her royal father had built a Palace on the site of a Hospice for Lepers—but she had never felt at home in it. Watching the looking-glass for fear of a sudden stiletto, the summer before she had seen a boy trifling with a girl under the hawthorn; she had smashed it with her jewelled sword into a thousand pieces. In the last year of her reign it was replaced.

Nowadays as the sun rises, the Horse Guards, the War Office and Westminster Abbey grow solidly grey; to the south, over Duck Island, Big Ben strikes the hour; ahead, the first light catches the gilt cross above St. Paul's. This is the moment of the birds' waking; this was the moment that another Queen found more wonderful than any other. After State Balls, she would come on to the portico of her Palace, as conscious of Prince Albert asleep on a sofa as she was conscious of the golden ring which he had placed on her finger ten years before. He had never liked the capital, preferring the life at Windsor or Balmoral. Yet for the Queen, she found this half mile of the Mall with its double rows of plane trees 'unsurpassed in grandeur'. Here at dawn she would watch the lark rise, just as later when she was a widow she would watch the couples trudge, their fingers irrevocably clasped, so that only the approaching thunder of hooves would cause them to jump aside, their arms still linked. She remembered how on this portico, in a manner that indicated rain, Lord Melbourne would say: 'Ma'am, the rooks are flying low. The rooks are my delight.' He had the patience to follow them by the score; she had the patience, but not the time . . .

So here are a scattered handful of views of the same scene. They are divided in time by not only three centuries, but by the influence of Le Nôtre on landscape gardening in the Sixteenth Century and by Nash in the early Nineteenth. In the vast library about London, woodcuts or tinted prints give as much the key to publication dates as the texts which they illustrate. Again, as each story is taken up by a new generation of chroniclers, so the texts are edited, re-written, and sometimes streamlined; gradually the photographer's art takes precedence over the engraver's. A study of park photography over the last twenty years can prove revealing.

By and large, until ten years ago, they were the usual postcard panoramas—a keeper feeding the pelicans on the Lake; Trooping the Colour; the triumphal return after the State Opening of Parliament. Now the accent is shifting from straight views to interpretative vision—a woman beneath an improvised sunshade of newspaper; a bank holiday crowd; or a toddler looking up questioningly at a sentry. There is a hint of caricature, just as a hint of caricature crept into the Victorian prints—a case of penny plain or tuppence coloured.

This shift of emphasis, I submit, may be attributed partly to the gathering influence of the cinema. Although a documentary feature has yet to be made about the parks, they so frequently serve as backgrounds to films that they have come to be accepted as the Old Kent Road or the lions at Trafalgar Square are accepted as backgrounds for the music-hall artist. In both cases, the focus is on the actor; the lens of the camera resembles the spotlight. For instance, the competitions in summer magazines illustrate the present craze for showing familiar objects, scenes and people from unfamiliar angles. Likewise, the cinema has affected the amateur with his ciné-camera. Naturally, there are still those who wish to film the Changing of the Guard, but there are many more who, crouching low, try to gain a strange perspective of a guardsman's busby. Again, copied from the art of the short feature, there are the more adventurous who, with the aid of time-exposure, shorten the hours and days of gestation so that the petals bursting from a bud, or the change from caterpillar to chrysalis, can take place in a few seconds. The director who knows the value of telescoping time has often served his apprenticeship with the short feature. Thus when he comes to his first full-length picture, he knows the value of *montage*. A shot of a sceptre may be followed by a crowbar; in the right context, the insinuation may be of a king looting monastic treasure. If the same shot were repeated at intervals until eventually the crowbar broke in a heavily studded chest, then the insinuation might be the fall of a king or protector. This is the visual language of comparison by association —a language not unlike the use to which the first Elizabethans put allegory.

In 1598, a German paused at an entrance to the Park to stop and copy the Latin inscription which he saw by Storey's Gate. Two centuries later, Horace Walpole came across Hentzer's correspondence and translated it. Here is his version of the Latin:

The fisherman who has been wounded learns, though late, to beware—
But the unfortunate Actaeon always presses on.
     The chaste virgin naturally pitied,
But the powerful goddess revenged the wrong.
     Let Actaeon fall a prey to his dogs,
          An example to youth,
A disgrace to those that belong to him!
May Dian live, the care of Heaven,
     The delight of mortals,
The security of those that belong to her.

When this version was issued at Walpole's private press in Strawberry Hill, he had to point out the clues to the allegory; that 'the fisherman' was Philip II, 'the disgrace' the defeat of the Armada. Yet originally the verse had been sent home by a foreign traveller without comment. The sting was as obvious as if a younger son today were to send his father in Alabama a picture of a negro walking with a white girl outside Marlborough House.

To speak, therefore, of St. James's is to be conscious that not only is it both the most photographed and filmed park in the capital, but also that it is both the most filmed and photographed because its palaces of Whitehall, St. James and Buckingham have endowed it in the eyes of the world with the most obvious attributes of royalty. Yet unlike Kensington Gardens, Hampton Court or Greenwich Park, no single book has been devoted to its history: an odd gap in the vast library about London.

So it is that in darkened rooms in New Orleans lie buried away on a few hundred feet of film the memories of all-night vigils kept to see royal processions pass; or, in the balmy air of a patio in Seville, the faint whirr of the reel unwinding may add its own commentary to the Crown birds as they nest each spring. For these royal associations lend St. James's Park a cosmopolitan quality. Beatrice Curtis Brown, exiled in America during the last war, in a charming book of memoirs writes of the *oriental* Whitehall backdrop of domes, minarets and towers. More recently, in a beautifully written pamphlet-guide commissioned by the Ministry of Works, Richard Church finds in St. James's an *Eastern* touch, as of a willow plate, heightened by the presence of the mandarin ducks and pelicans on the Lake.

One is the voice of a poet at home, the other of a temporary exile. Yet it is the voice of the Old World speaking from the New which at first is the more striking. Absence makes the heart grow fonder and home is where the heart is: these are the simple truths of universal belief; but in the New World they undergo a certain re-orientation. On the other side of the Atlantic, there are American-Chinese and American-Irish communities, just as there are American-Dutch and American-Slav colonies: yet, in every case, nationalization as subjects of the United States has made them one hundred per cent American in their allegiances.

This is a process which has been going on for over fifty years and, whenever it is conveniently forgotten, that is generally because other nations have become poorer and there is a natural tendency to despise richer relations. Yet the truth remains that if emigrants from all nationalities can find themselves thus absorbed by the New World, it is never to a full forgetting of the Old. In New York, 'a platter of spaghetti' or 'a pitcher of water' are restaurant phrases recalling Seventeenth Century England; they have become absorbed as living relics into the growing language. For it is sometimes just too easy to smile at the crop-head as he swings his camera round the Victoria Memorial in preparation for taking a long shot of the Mall. When he says in a broad accent, 'Gee! this is history,' it is sometimes just too tempting to condemn him for a certain un-English naïveté. When France was set free by the Allies and the American tanks drove down the Champs Elysées, it was hard for Tommies, with their instinctive reserve, to understand why some G.Is. wept. 'It's the beauty,' I heard a simple boy from Virginia whimper; it was a fresh, spontaneous reaction. Were the action to be repeated now, he would be described as 'a mixed-up kid'—so widely has America's financial prosperity bred an envy in less prosperous lands. Yet nations are like Malvolio—some achieve greatness; some are born great; and some have greatness thrust upon them. America is in the position of being a new Malvolio—with a cross gartering of all three. Her tourists to the Mall have as much to give as to learn.

For the Mall in its history has seen sovereigns and presidents and royalty of every nation. Had a camera been fixed with a time-exposure, it might have recorded some strange ironies—or *montages*. There would have been reigns when the vanquished of one generation would be driving with the victors of the next; there would have been centuries when the great sweep would have resembled a musical ride, with the partners of one alliance changing mounts to dance with the next. Yet had the camera been there when this was still sumpy ground, frequently overflowed by the Thames, there would have been found about the dense forests and woods of Westminster a people of small tribes whose unification years later still shows in its sympathy for the underdog, or that cross-gartering of Saxon, Celtic and Cymric strands that so loves to claim an ancestry somewhere over the hills and far away. Perhaps for landsmen an immortal longing of which the sea and air are symbols, or perhaps for townsmen a longing of which the parks and gardens in their cities are an explanation.

II

S T. JAMES THE GREAT and St. James the Less are the patrons of pilgrims, and the history of the London park sharing their name has been largely associated with pilgrimage. This may be an obvious thing to say; the curiosity is that it is so seldom remembered. . . .

. . . So to go back to the beginning is to return to the time when St. James's Fields were no more than a series of islands, lost in the high-river tides. To the Saxons of the reign of King Offa, there existed simply dense woodland and dark pools, just as centuries before to the Romans the whole of Britain had seemed no more than a series of islands, lost in the blackness of northern seas. One was the immediate view, the other that of conquerors believing that they had reached the *ultima thule*. But such was not the case with the tribes who lived on this flat edge of the world: over the hills, across the water and towards the setting sun, they dreamed of islands as uncharted as their own. That these dreams have been a constant factor down the ages is an inheritance which the first invading Legions bred. How that inheritance has endured can be measured by the excitement still caused when a piece of coloured tile is discovered, or when the names of rosemary, parsley, sage, Christmas rose, lavender, spearmint, periwinkle or Madonna Lily are remembered in their original Latin.

Roman plants and Roman law—both have survived; the barbarian may have broken the pavements of villa and temple, but he could no more destroy the flowers of which the tessellated paving were emblems than he could destroy the law which flowered from such a civilization. Possibly a thousand years hence some of the English gardens laid out in the Calcutta of Warren Hastings, or the seed of yellow mullein now flown to the wives of Civil Servants in Jamaica, will similarly evoke memories of Mountbatten's handing over of self-government to India, or some of the South Pacific comedies of Noël Coward. For

142

home from home has ever been the unwritten order of every colonial service, be it Roman, Norman or British. For in Britain it would appear that her peninsulas, abundant waterways and fretted coasts are characteristics which have become reflected in her people, engendering in them a steady pull between love of home and adventure in some foreign field 'that is for ever England'. In men such as Drake or Captain Cook, it reached the masthead; yet at every level it can be found—on the liners packed with emigrants bound for Melbourne as once when the same decks had been packed with troops bound for Malta, Malaya or St. Malo.

When the Romans sailed away for the last time in the Fourth Century, they left behind them *Londinium*, a noble City of brick and Kentish ragstone, clustering north of the river, one of the nine *coloniae* of the country and third only in importance to *Verulamium* (St. Albans) or *Eboracum* (York). Two Temples marked the future sites of Westminster Abbey and St. Paul's Cathedral—the first dedicated to Apollo, the second to Diana. Later, a future Dean of St. Paul's was to write to the Dean of Westminster to say that he must produce 'an image of Apollo as like that of Belvedere as his to the Dian of the Louvre' and that then, and only then, might the Abbey compete with the Cathedral for 'antiquity of heathen worship'. The Dean of Westminster of the time retorted that his Temple of Apollo had been swallowed by an earthquake. This reply is taken by some as a dodging of proof positive, while others accept it as a legend. I veer towards this second interpretation.

Not only is it known that storms were much more violent, say, in the Sixth rather than the Sixteenth Century, but legends never spring from nowhere. Somewhere there exists a basis of fact, however slight. Caesar in his account of Britain speaks of her people being ruled by stones, by which he means presumably that they were subject to a pagan priesthood whose rites were carried out on high ground surrounded by stones, or in avenues lined with stones. These rites were doubtless a form of nature worship. Certainly, nature worship has left its mark on local industries such as folk weaving and spinning, where a mathematical concern with stitches carries with it a magic sense of numbers as well as a sense of the elemental—although in the beginning, when the Empire first came into contact with the native priesthood, nature worship acquired another dimension—that of the supernatural (or unnatural, as some might add). There is something as decidedly elemental in a row of poplars as a row of pillars; to bow down before one is not so widely different from kneeling before the other. The Temple of Apollo may have stood on the site of Westminster Abbey—and it may have been swallowed in an earthquake. Yet whether this is fact or fiction, a truth resides in the legend—namely that this spot became hallowed because it was high and therefore dry ground suitable for worship.

Before *Londinium*, the name had been *Llyndin* or *Llyndun*. *Llyn* is of Celtic origin (pronounced *lun*) meaning a lake or pool—and hence the swampy nature of the first foundation, which is still preserved in that part beyond London Bridge described as 'the Pool'. Further, *din* or *dun* suggest a hill, high land, or a fortress; this could apply to the present Abbey site, St. Paul's, Cornhill or the Tower—or to all four. As late as the Twelfth Century the Abbey stood on an island. A profusion of thorns gave the place the name of Thorney, and the word island was added because a tributary breaking free from the Thames looped the church, providing it with a natural moat. The dryness of the spot had meant that men could kneel here, and, as its ring of water meant also that there could be no surprise attack, so there grew up the feeling of a sanctuary set apart. Later, when in 616, King Sebert of the East Saxons founded the first church here, the ground became consecrated.

However, on the eve of the consecration, there runs a story that St. Peter called a ferryman telling him to inform his bishop that the river would be rich with salmon provided that he and the other ferrymen remembered two things: 'first, that you never fish again on Sundays; second, that you pay a tithe of them to the Abbey'. This may be a legend (perhaps a profitable legend put out by an Abbot) though, whether this is the case or not, it testifies to another more important truth—the linking of superstition with the supernatural. To steal a fish without a tithe being paid, or to steal abroad early on a Sunday and catch a salmon, was to invite a run of bad luck; all day, in punishment the next week, a man might labour in vain with his nets and catch

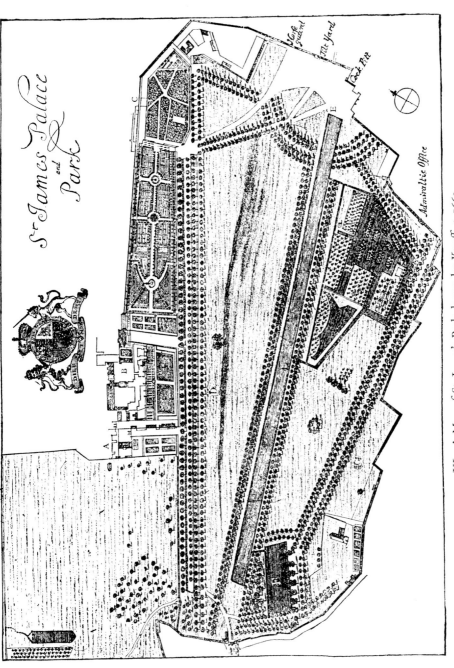

St James Palace and Park

XL. A Map of St. James's Park drawn by Knyff, c. 1662.

XLIB. Rosamond's Pond in 1740; an engraving made from a picture by Hogarth.

XLIA. The Mall in 1732; an engraving from the title-page to Walthoe's Edition of Lord Lansdowne's *Works*.

nothing. Yet the borderlines between superstition and the supernatural can at times be perilously near—especially in missionary countries such as the Britain of the Dark Ages. For to understand what happened between the departure of the Romans and the arrival of the Normans an understanding of those Dark Ages is essential. (If this seems a long preamble before coming back to the Park, subsequently I hope to show that these 'long shots' were necessary to my purpose, since, without them, the later 'close-ups' would appear unrelated and without sequence.)

Between the disintegration of the Empire and the Battle of Hastings, lie the Dark Ages. By the thousand, schoolboys are taught to believe that they led towards the light; they should be reminded that if they did lead towards the light, they were also dark because they had passed out of the light. To convert this metaphor into historical terms, when the Legions withdrew, Roman Law went underground; there followed the reign of the different barbarians so that, as the centuries progressed, so the people tended to look back to a golden age of justice and order; the memory of the Roman inheritance was sung at the communal fire. If a missionary Church had been established to carry on and develop that tradition of law, then in the transition her converts found themselves constantly open to attack by those raiding parties which would sail silently up the riverways of the country and plunder the towns; the more raids that succeeded, the bolder became the invaders, whereas for those who were plundered, the darker grew the horizons. King Arthur became a myth and was powerful as a myth because he defeated the pagan invaders—and when a myth became transformed into primitive art the new heroes and saints resembled the old mythical gods and heroes. Bishops would be drawn holding bunches of grapes—as Bacchus did, or St. George would be given a far-away look not unlike that of Perseus. As much as the Christians adopted and, as it were resurrected the Roman law from the English catacombs, so in proportion did the fame of the heroes of the Christian Church spread—Bede, Alfred, Dunstan. Yet during all this long dark period of transition there was growing in the towns and cities (Bede honoured London as 'the mart of many nations') the notion that forests, cut by Roman roads, were retreats offering food, game and

safety. In short, against the fear of attack, they offered centres of enchantment where men did not behave as beasts like the barbarians, but
where the beasts behaved like men. The myth of the Arthurian legend
had brought with it the myth of the enchanted forest—and from there
to the myth of the enchanted park was a short mediaeval step: St.
James's became such a park because of its geographical position; and
because its fields lay almost within the shadow of consecrated towers,
so more and more in the mind of its inhabitants did religion and
royalty become linked. Between the Abbey and Palace, a spell was
cast. But if spell is a word that is too closely associated with abraca-
dabra, then perhaps race-memory were better substituted.

By the slow progress of law it came to be assumed that this enchanted forest belonged to the Abbots of Westminster. Nobody ever
decreed that this was so—although, somewhere between the dates
606 and 1066, the prerogative to cut down trees passed into the hands
of the monks; thence forward to make a right of way without their
permission was to risk being 'cursed' as a trespasser; the woods became
holy places in which sanctuary might be sought—as in the Abbey.
Those who broke these rules did not do so under the fear of any fine,
but rather kept them for fear lest they might be punished in another
manner; there arose the superstition that to hunt without paying a
tithe on the takings was to steal from God and that to steal from God
might be to cut off supernatural help when a bear charged, or a dragon
roared. So it was that when Abbot Islip made a gift of most of this
land to Henry VII, these fields never lost their earlier religious, super-
stitious or enchanted character. I say fields advisedly, since after seven
centuries of systematic irrigation the ground had been drained and
only a few scattered copses recalled the Saxon scene in a Tudor
landscape.

From the beginning, there had been at the centre of this scene a
pool, which by some was described as a lake—although at the time
when the change from ecclesiastical to royal tenure took place there
occurred also a change of name. Cowford Pool was henceforth
referred to as Rosamond's Pond. This sheet of water, which was
subsequently turned into a Canal by Le Nôtre and by Nash into the
present artificial Lake, was fed by the Tyburn, when that stream was

known as the Eia-burn because it ran past the Estate of Eia (Hyde Park) and when that Estate reached as far east as Hay Hill. In Cockney, Hay Hill is still sometimes called 'Eye Hill', and Eye-brook is a bastard of the family of Eya-burne or Eye-burn from whose contraction comes Th'Eyeburn whence Tyburn. It was this stream that made its way into Green Park (when it was known as an Upper St. James's Park) and from there through Cowford to the Thames, about a furlong west of today's Vauxhall Bridge.

Of the name Cowford as little is known as of the derivation of Rosamond's Pond. Some have thought that it may have referred to a cow which stumbling into the marshy ground finally drowned herself —possibly in the Eighth Century—because it is then that the name first appears. Its significance for the Park is that it is to be found in charters just about the time that the name of St. James is introduced.

After two centuries of felling trees and making firm causeways between the pools (the forest yielded enough pannage to feed a hundred hogs), there lay a huge swampy meadow north of the monastic property. Here a hospital was founded by fourteen maidens 'that were leprous'. They were maidens in the true sense and so quite naturally decided to put themselves under the patronage of that Apostle and Nazarite 'who was also a virgin'. Their life was to be as dedicated as a nun's, and 'to live chastely and honestly in divine service' is how the chroniclers have described their rule. They wished to emulate St. James the Less of whom it was told by St. Jerome that he prostrated himself so much in prayer that 'the skin of his knees and forehead were hardened like a camel's hoofs'. Six chaplains and two laymen were appointed to look after their spiritual and physical needs. As the Sisterhood grew, they became remembered in wills, and by the reign of Edward the Confessor they were farming some one hundred and sixty acres around their hospital and had been left the revenue of eighty acres between Hampstead and Hendon. The generosity of the dead called forth a rival generosity from the living King; he decreed that a fair be held on St. James's eve which should last five days; the profits should be given to the Sisterhood and, to increase those profits, a public holiday should be proclaimed for a week during which all the stalls in the City should be shut down.

Reference will be found to this fair beginning on the 24th July, the vigil of St. James the Great. Yet the hospital was dedicated to St. James the Less, whose feast falls on the 2nd May. The confusion springs from the fact that both were martyred—one by the sword, the other by the club—and that painters and historians, no less than kings and queens, have muddled the two weapons and hence the two stories. Invocation to each has been about equal in measure, and at this stage in the history of London's oldest royal park, perhaps it were more gracious to accept a human error of dates as a double blessing in disguise.

Between the Leper Hospital and the Eya Stream stood the Eya Cross. When Abbot Islip had annexed a hundred acres of monastic property in 1531, this Cross featured in the deeds as a boundary corner-stone. Here the first Norman Kings held their *placita* or public courts, reminders of *jours de mai* in their own country—although, by the reign of Edward the Confessor, it was more frequently used by the chaplains attached to the hospital as 'a preaching stone'. Here each June, competing against the sound of pipe and tabor, they would address the crowds on their way to the fair. Charity was their text—the charity that is the leach of life and abides. . . . Frequently today on the lawns of houses bordering the south of the Park, against the tinkle of tea-cups in marquees, vicars will come to open fêtes in aid of boys' orphan-ages, or homes for the aged.[1] Charity is their text—the charity that is more than a bazaar commodity and abideth. Yet in their speeches, as in those of their predecessors in the Twelfth Century, the blessing of St. James the Less on patrons is as much invoked as that of St. James the Great.

When Henry VIII grew impatient to move such 'a leprous eyesore' from the view backing his Palace at Westminster, he also knew how politic it was to compensate the Sisterhood. Before him, Henry IV had put the hospice under the protection of Eton College, and now the new King arranged with the Governors that in lieu of their West-minster Fields they should be given Chatisham and other properties in

[1] An interesting print by George Scharf shows a fête (1830) being run to raise funds for Charing Cross Hospital in one of these back gardens: unfortunately it proved too blurred a picture to reproduce.

Suffolk. To one of the sisters, Jane Harwood, he decreed that she should be granted an annual pension of £6. 1s. 4d.

Thus it was that on the foundation of St. James's Hospice for Lepers was founded St. James's Palace; moreover, the King had thrown a lassoo to bring within his London hunting grounds a loop of land reaching as far north as Highgate and Hampstead. Within five years Parliament countered with an Act whereby the limits of 'the royal palaces in Westminster' were restricted. This Act mentions 'a park, walled and environed with brick and stone, and therein . . . devised many and singular commodious things, pleasures and other necessaries'. These necessaries referred to stocking the ground with deer, 'laying out a tilting yard', and making a bowling alley.

In the State Papers of 1572 there appears the Office of 'Keeper of the Ponds in the Park of Westminster', and reference is again made to these ponds in the second year of the reign of James I when His Majesty ordered £400 to be paid for bringing 'a current of water from Hyde Park, in a vault arched over to fall into Rosamond's Pond, with other charges for making and clearing the head of the said pond and cleaning the passages and sluices'. The salary of the Keeper was doubled this year to £12. 13s. 4d. Two years later, the Pond was 'scoured', but all this operation consisted of was re-building the banks with fresh mud and draining and re-filling the basin with fresh water. As soon as this was completed, another order went out to weed and cut nettles; soon, too, the eastern promontory was famous for lovers. Yet hardly had the season of the courtiers' progress and the farmers' profit reached May than the proverb 'as you make your bed so must you lie on it' acquired a more stinging edge. For the nettles came back in full strength and this promontory became a veritable nettle-bed. A gardener was now dispatched not to scythe the nettles as had been done before, but to uproot each one, singly. By the season of plums and pears, when the buck is ready to be hunted and the spaniel a trained retriever for the partridge, the scene had acquired a pastoral quality. In comparison with the glitter and twitter of court etiquette, life in the Park seemed enchanted and idyllic. In the long grass, while the bee and the ant made winter provision, the bells of the City would ring their hourly quatrain:

All through this hour
Lord be my guide.
And by thy power
No foot shall slide.

The haymakers would be in these Fields building stacks, the swans in
their woody islets, and a few early fires would send their trails of
smoke above poplar and willow to mark the village of Charing. A
royal poet, turning on his side, shading his eyes with his hat, might be
thinking of love spurned and his mistress whose heart lay like a green
leaf closed in a book. But find the page, but find the page . . . and
scampering over the meadows a boy would come running with the
news that the King's hunting party had returned and awaited this
jester's cheer.

James I was as fond of hunting and sport as any of his predecessors:
he had many pets and they in turn observed their own aristocracy.
'Greyhounds, Spaniels and Hounds . . . whereof the first might seem
the Lords, the second the Gentlemen, and the last the Yeomen of
dogs.' The Park was a royal Arcadia—though even in an Arcadia
everything must have its appointed place. There is a royalty of nature
to be kept in which the mongrel must give way to the thoroughbred,
or Clarabel expect to be milked before Cowslip.

The Duke of Buckingham, with more loyalty than knowledge of
geography, had hoped to bring back to his sovereign a lion from
Madrid (there were lions in the rival menagerie in the Tower.) But he
was unsuccessful, only sending in advance of him a report that might
act as some compensation.

Four asses you I have sent. Tow hees and shees. Five camels, tow hees with
a young one; and one ellefant which is your worth seeing. These I have
impudently begged for you. There is a Barbarie hors comes with them, I
think for Wat Aston. My Lord Bristow [the Ambassador in Spain] sayeth
he will send you more camels. When we come ourselves we will bringe you
horses and asses enoufe. If I know whether you desire mules or not I will
bringe them, or deere of this countrie eyther. And I will lay waite for all the
rare coler birds that can be herd of.

Yet the news of this menagerie in the Park had spread. The House of
Savoy sent a leopard, which, alas, fell into instant disgrace on its

arrival by attacking a favourite fawn; the Great Mogul sent two antelopes; the Czar of Muscovy sent live sables and hawks (he had heard with amazement in the first year of the reign how birds had frozen in mid-air during the Great Frost to drop like stones on the fields below.) A certain Captain Newport presented a wild boar, and the Virginia Company some flying squirrels: other assorted gifts included crocodiles, ducks, and cormorants specially trained for use in fishing. These were all housed in separate ponds near the Vine Garden attached to the Palace.

The elephant cost £273 to board; his keeper was paid a salary of £250 a year and insisted that his charge be given a gallon of wine every morning during the winter months. In Peacham's list of remarkable sights, prefixed in Coryatt's *Crudities* of 1611, here are three representative lines:

> St. James' his guinea hens, the Cassowary, moreover
> The beaver in the Park (strange beast as ever any man saw,
> Down shearing-willows, with teeth as sharp as handsaw).

According to a footnote in the original edition, a cassowary is 'an East India bird . . . that will carry no coales, but eat them as hot as you will'. Evelyn in his diaries also speaks of this bird—as does Mr. Moncony who spells as though he suffered from a stutter. 'A quessa-ouarroe' reads his version.

The King heartily disliked the Tower—but the promise of seeing performing lions would ever draw him there. In 1604, appropriately enough he visited Lion Tower to see a battle between a lion, a lioness, and a cock. Five years later, he went with the Prince of Wales to watch a fight between a bear 'doomed to punishment' because it had killed a child, and a lion noted for its ferocity. Alack, once in the arena, the ferocious lion did not feel inclined to spring and ignominiously retreated to his cage—as did every other lion that afternoon; in the end, 'to humour His Majesty', the dogs were allowed to bait the bear to death.

Bear-baiting has been compared to bull-fighting; there have been frequent exchanges between English and Spanish travellers, each finding an inconsistency in his censorship of the other. Now that bear-baiting no longer continues and cock-fighting is technically illegal (there are still several unofficial pits in the North), the opponents of bull-fighting have tended to bracket it with fox-hunting, vivisection and circuses. These are crank causes, it is sometimes said—, and if by this is meant causes on the periphery of normal life, then there is sometimes a tendency to forget that at the centre there must be some form of blood-letting. Now and again the world needs a blood-bath—such is the verdict of Blimpery. Yet perhaps it hides a truth which in times of peace finds its expression at the bull-ring, as once it did at the bear-pit—or in fox-hunting or a girl spinning from the Big Top, her life in her teeth. In all these acts, there is something sacrificial, just as in any public execution by the State there still remains the note of the protracted ritual sacrifice: the sentence passed, the fading hopes of reprieve, the last choice of a meal. 'Is it right that one just man should die for the good of many?' Sometimes it is even right, for there is a sense in which the victim, be he innocent or guilty, must serve as a scapegoat—though the irony is that a feeling of guilt is often transferred to his executioners as for instance when the law demands that after a hangman has pursued his trade, he must be acquitted by a private jury of his deed. The rule of scapegoats is that as one goes, so another must be found. Or put another way, when the cat o' nine tails is laid aside or the number of executions decrease, then the path is made clear for crank societies such as those that in the name of religion would protest against men playing cricket on a Sunday, or a Queen's Consort from taking part in a polo match. There have ever been these nigglers—the Bible is full of warnings against them—, and under the Protectorship, when the *Saint* was dropped from James's Park, fines were imposed for breaking the silence of the Sabbath by playing either the flute or viol upon the lawns. Yet many of those who now enforced these laws were among those who had danced the lavolta or corantoe in the reign before: they were the time-servers, typical in any period, who blow hot one moment, cold the next, and whose censures on the chastity of others mounts in exact proportion to the decrease of charity in themselves.

If King James I lived the life of a full-blooded monarch with as much passion for hunting as collecting animals in his menagerie, then it was with a particular preference for animals of a royalty of nature such as the lion. In Elizabethan and Jacobean England, bears seem to have been considered inferior animals. 'The bear wants a tail and cannot be a lion', and it is perhaps not being wise after the event to ascribe this sentiment of Thomas Fuller to an attitude of mind that was even prevalent in Shakespeare's day:

> Like to a choas, or an unlick'd bear-whelp
> That carries no impression like the dam.

For maybe it was the shapelessness of the bear at birth, as opposed to the lion cub, that brought about this attitude. Perforce the mother bear must lick her child into shape, all that is prominent at birth being claws —and maybe it was this precise formlessness in the beginning which subsequently created the prejudice against the grown animal. For long before the habit of baiting had grown, there was a prejudice against the animal—as witness the anonymous Fourteenth Century spiritual treatise, *The Cloud of Unknowing*. Yet before I develop this point later, let me end with the observation that whereas the dancing bear in a muzzle and skirt looks a fool there is still something magnificent about the lion that leaps through a hoop of flame.

Lions are partial to lavender. This piece of folklore recalls 'Lord' George Sanger's telling comment: 'Lions are all right if they're spoken to respectful like.'

'Lavender, who'll buy my sweet lavender', was a familiar cry of the Eighteenth, Nineteenth and early Twentieth Centuries. David Jones, the painter and writer, records how his grandmother was always saddened at this cry, which she associated with August and the end of summer. In some very lonely places in England 'to lay in lavender' means to pawn—a relic from Ben Jonson's day when clothes pawned were said to lie in lavender to keep them sweet. Lavender was grown in profusion at Hitchin during the Fifteenth and Sixteenth Centuries, and it was used by herbal doctors in Wales as early as the Thirteenth. Near St. James's Palace, a Physic Garden was developed because the King was particularly interested in the medicinal and herbal qualities of plants.

The same interest, though not in lions, was inherited by his son, Charles I. Monsieur de la Serre, attached to the Court of Queen Henrietta, refers slightingly to this Physic Garden; he then goes on to consider the Park itself, which he finds 'planted with divers avenues of trees, and covered with the shade of an innumerable number of oaks, whose old age renders them very agreeable, as it makes them impervious to the beams of the sun'. He concludes: 'This Park is full of wild animals, but as it is the place where the ladies of the Court usually take their walk, their kindness has made the animals so tame, that they all submit to the power of their charms rather than to the pursuit of the dogs.'

That there was decline in the upkeep of the Palace Gardens and the Park between the reign of James I and Charles II is testified by other foreign visitors. Indeed, during the period of the Commonwealth, Parliament had to order that the Park be re-stocked with deer from Bushy and Hampton Court. This re-stocking was paid for by the sale of the deer in Hyde Park for £300—an early example of bureaucracy, when much time, trouble and expense could have been saved by simply driving the deer from one park to the other. Further, the fact that the deer were vanishing from St. James's, suggests a slackness on the part of the rangers—a fact further borne out by the gradual disappearance of the menagerie until, by the time of the Restoration, Charles II had to begin all over again—only this time he let the emphasis fall on birds.

Yet before turning to his decoy for catching wild fowl, which the King had set on Duck Island, or the derivation of the name Birdcage Walk, there are three popular stories to be discountenanced. They concern Charles I, Cromwell and Charles II. 'Copperfield, do you recollect the date?' Mr. Dick's question has a relevance for all three. So first, King Charles's head. . . .

On the way to his execution, with a regiment of footguards before and after him, bare-headed the King made his way accompanied by the beating of drums. At the opening into Spring Gardens (i.e. the present King Charles Street) he is supposed to have pointed to some trees, begging that they be as well tended by the gardeners of the Republic as they had been by his own men. This was a part of Royalist propaganda—a means of showing the Sovereign's disregard of imminent death. Similarly the Ministry of Information during the last war issued tales of Spitfire pilots finishing rounds of cards before climbing into their cockpits, just as Drake had finished his game of bowls before sailing: that both these stories are actually true only emphasized the kind of truth at which the Royalists were driving in 1640—a truth in which death had no sting. Yet Colonel Tomlinson, 'who had charge of the King' on this walk, reports that he discoursed only on things 'touching his burial', the which he prayed the Duke of Richmond and others 'to take care of'.

Again, with the death of Cromwell, it is a case of 'do you recollect the date?' On the 3rd September, 1658, the Lord Protector died. Foster in his book, *Statesmen of the Commonwealth*, declared that on the 2nd September a mighty storm blew, reaching as far south as the shipping in the Mediterranean. It was a night in London such as had rarely been passed 'by dwellers in crowded streets'. Trees were torn from their roots, chimneys blown down, houses unroofed: 'it was indeed a night which prophesied woeful times to England—[though] to Cromwell it proved a night of happiness'. For 'it ushered in for him, far more surely than Worcester or Dunbar, his Fortunate Day'. Waller provided some lines for the occasion:

> Heaven his great soul doth claim,
> In storms as loud as his immortal fame.
> His dying groans, his last breath shakes, our isle,
> And trees uncut fall for his funeral pile:
> About his palace their broad roots are tost
> Into the air. So Romulus was lost!

But all nature is double and there are two ways of looking at everything; the water that drowns also cleanses—and Waller was quickly answered:

> The winds were all let loose to blow the fire;
> For quick descent of the blood-guilty ghost,
> Earth threw her entrails up, their roots trees tost;
> The nightbird waiting till the dying tone,
> Despair breath'd in a dismal mandrake's groan:
> Though some, to elevate his guilt, maintain
> That sank not Charon but the hurricane.

There the matter might have ended. Unfortunately in each case, Roundhead and Cavalier, the date of the storm had been altered to fit their sentiments. No less than both poets, the historian sinned as much. There was a freak summer storm in 1658, but it did not occur in September. Before August was out, it had died away.

With these two examples, the death of Charles I and Cromwell, I have sometimes wondered if Dickens (who in passing was no mean historian of the parks) had not also tumbled on the hard facts. When he was creating the character of Mr. Dick, perhaps they lay buried, but mounted subconsciously in that oddly surrealist speech in which Mr. Dick confuses his own head with that of Charles I. ' "There's plenty of string," he said, unwinding the kite, "and when it flies high, it takes the facts a long way. That is my manner of diffusing 'em. I don't know where they may come down. It's according to circumstances, and the wind, and so forth; but I take my chance on that." '[1]

'I take my chance on that.' How well the motto becomes the writer of London's topography, who tries to break through the confusion and conflict of views about both Le Nôtre's contribution to the Park and Charles II's part in laying out Birdcage Walk.

Le Nôtre was certainly invited to St. James's Palace by the King: of that, there is conclusive proof from laundry bills. Further, on seeing the Park, he said that he neither wished it changed into a Bois de Boulogne nor an imitation of the Tuileries Gardens: of that, too, there is conclusive proof in contemporary letters. Yet there were changes, carried out by Royal Command, and I am tempted to take my chance on the view that, although Le Nôtre did not bring these about in the sense that he was in control of the gardeners, nonetheless he had the King's ear so that when the gardeners were ordered to rearrange the landscape they were acting at one remove from suggestions first made by the French architect. Anyway, all these changes were for the better.

Le Nôtre (anglicized by some as Lenotre) is indirectly mentioned in a volume, published in Cologne in 1727, and purporting to be the correspondence of a Swiss gentleman: 'I have been told the King wished to render St. James's . . . more beautiful, and for that purpose summoned from Paris a clever man.' The writer continues: '. . . this man was of the opinion that the natural simplicity of this Park, its rural and in some places wild character, had something more grand than he

[1] See p. 184 also.

could impart to it'. The 1727 editor of these letters believed them to have been written thirty years before publication—some time in the mid-1690s. If this were so, the Swiss gentleman would be working from memory, there being a time-gap of some further thirty years between his recalling of Le Nôtre's visit to St. James's and his putting of pen to paper.

Another strand of thought may be picked up from *London Past and Present*, published in 1850. Here the editor plumps for Dr. Morison as the King's chief adviser in re-planning the Park and refers his readers for confirmation to the correspondence of a Dr. Worthington, issued by the Chetham Society. The only reference that can be traced to this Dr. Morison reads: '[Mr. Wray] tells me of one Dr. Morison, that hath care of the great garden now preparing in St. James's. . . .' Now, in 1660, Dr. Morison was appointed to the office of botanical physician and head herbalist, which makes me suspect that the reference in the Chetham papers must be to the Physic Garden, which had existed from James I's reign. In this, my reading tallies with Larwood.

What changes there were, lessened neither the rustic charm of the Park nor its enchantment. Yet from now on the word enchantment has to be used with qualification: coupled with it henceforth must go a sense of the exotic. 'The pools were linked into a river', Pepys records, and in his entry for the 16th September, 1660, he notes that three hundred men were at work on the task. Yet the natural springs were insufficient to feed this project and a subterranean channel had to be burrowed between the Thames and a sluice gate that opened on the far side of the Parade Ground. Pepys however was thought a little old-fashioned in referring to it as 'a river'; it was called instead the Canal because there was thought to be an artificial enchantment about a canal (Plate XL, facing p. 144)—an enchantment such as still exists in the canvas caverns down which the boats of a fairground bump their way from grotto to grotto.

Robert Waller, whose clothes were as reversible as his politics, now turned a coat of sackcloth into one of courtly blue; he bade his Muse stay while he wrote of 'beauteous Rosamond . . . that noted pond . . . to which the happy shes sometimes repair'. Or as a prophet new inspired, he turned towards the Canal to watch—

> a shoal of silver fishes glide,
> And play around the gilded barge's side;
> The ladies angling in the crystal lake,
> Feast on the waters on the prey they take,
> At once victorious with their lines and eyes,
> They make the fishes and the men their prize.

But these were lines of poetic licence rather than truth, for although the King swam here, there were neither boats nor gilded barges. Not until the late Nineteenth Century did the sound of the concertina echo across this Ornamental Water as clerks pulled on the oars of their wherries.

South of the Canal, west of Storey's Gate, ran Birdcage Walk. The name is something of a mystery. It is commonly supposed to have sprung from the fact that here the King had the cages of his favourite birds hung from the trees. Larwood could never find any proof of this in the prints of the time, nor have I been any more fortunate in my researches; it is odd, too, that this aspect should have been overlooked when so much else has been so scrupulously recorded. So again I must take my chance with Mr. Dick—only this time on 'Lord' George Sanger whose seventy years as a showman coincided with Dickens' whole writing life (Kenneth Grahame always hoped that the novelist had been at one of those roadside audiences—a happy thought).[1] As quite a small boy, George decided to begin his life as an animal trainer. 'I went to some dealers in what was then known as Birdcage Walk, in Bethnal Green, and purchased five hen canaries, two redpoles, and six white mice.' Such was his first troupe.

Birdcage Walk in Bethnal Green no longer exists—though there are those who can just remember it. They tell me that the dealers who served Sanger were in the habit of selling their birds indoors during the winter, so that it is possible that likewise Charles II had his exotic birds kept indoors in the houses that ran along the southern boundary of his Park. The story of the cages hanging from the trees may have applied only to the hottest days in summer. Moreover, as every so often a painter will dismiss a picture from ever reaching a canvas with the excuse that the light will not be the same the next day, so perhaps

[1] Grahame wrote an introduction to the 1926 reprint of Sanger's book.

the illustrators of the Restoration may have used the same excuse with regard to the birds. For the odd thing is that they were prolific enough in drawing the Walk but not the cages. Yet of the Royal Aviary and Duck Island there is abundant proof—in prints; in poems; and in journals.[1]

Rosamond's Pond, to the west of the Palace, remained untouched. A sluice had been burrowed to connect it with the Canal and so link it to the Thames, and now that the Puritan régime had ended, it once more became the favoured resort of lovers. The plays of Congreve, Farquhar and Otway are full of allusions to it—as indeed is Sedley's *Mulberry Garden*, a Restoration Comedy which borrowed its name and setting from a plantation of mulberry trees that James I had laid out, north of Rosamond's Pond, on the present site of Buckingham Palace. A Cheesecake House stood in the centre; on a clear day, too, Storey's Gate could be seen—though often it was obscured by mists thought to be caused by the swampy ground. So the King had hay-seed sown, thus hoping to reclaim such marshy territory. In this he succeeded only to discover that the mists were caused by the sea-coal burnt in the Westminster breweries.

Of Duck Island, Evelyn provides a delightful account:

I went to St. James' . . . where I saw various animals, and examined the throat of the *Onocrotylus*, or pelican, a fowl between a stork and a swan, a melancholy water-fowl, brought from Astracan by the Russian Ambassador. It was diverting to see how he would toss up and turn a flat fish, plaice or flounder, to get it right into his gullet at its lower beak, which, being filmy stretches to a prodigious wideness when it devours a great fish. Here also was a small waterfowl, not bigger than a moorhen, that went almost quite erect, like the penguin of America; it would eat as much fish as its whole body weighed; I never saw so unsatiable a devourer, yet the body did not appear to swell the bigger. The Solan Geese here are also great devourers, and are said to exhaust all the fish in the pond. Here was a curious sort of poultry, not much exceeding the size of a tame pigeon, with legs so short as their crops seemed to touch the earth; a milk-white raven; a stork, which was a rarity at the season, seeing he was loose, and to fly loftily; two Balearian cranes, one of which having had one of his legs broken and cut off above the knee, had a wooden or boxen leg and thigh, with a joint so accurately made,

[1] This paragraph may savour of special pleading. The explanation I offer is a poor one, I know, but I cannot think of a better and must leave it at that.

that the creature could walk and use it as well as if it had been natural; it was made by a soldier. The Park was at this time stored with numerous flocks of several sorts of ordinary and extraordinary wild fowl, breeding about the decoy, which for being near so great a city, and among such a concourse of soldiers and people, is a singular and diverting thing. . . . There were withy-pots or nests, for the wild fowl to lay their eggs in, a little above the surface of the water.

There is something particularly English about a Balearian crane being fitted with a wooden leg by a soldier; it has the same quality of eccentricity as the once overheard complaint of an elderly lady in a poultry shop: 'That bird you sold me was a cripple.' Or I am reminded of those appeals sometimes put up on area railings, seeking homes for new kittens, or of the notice I once saw pinned to a house in Queen Anne's Gate:

FOUND
YOUNG BLACK
SHORT-HAIRED
TOM CAT
Apply Within

Such notices, only for dogs, were frequently pinned to the trees of the Park after the Restoration. Here is one entry, which having been up three days, then found its way into the *London Gazette*, during November, 1761. 'Lost four or five days in St. James's . . . a Dog of His Majesty, full of blue spots, with a white cross on his forhead, and about the bigness of a tumbler.' Another, a longer notice from the *Mercurius Politicus*, reads: 'We must call upon you again for a black dog, between a greyhound and a spaniel, no white about him, only a streak on his Brest, and Tayl a little bobbed. It is His Majesty's own dog, and doubtless was stolen, for the Dog was not born nor bred in England and would never forsake his Master. Whosoever finds him may acquaint him at Whitehall, for his Dog was better at Court than those who stole him. Will they never leave robbing His Majesty? Must he not keep a Dog? This Dog's place (though better than some imagine) is the only place which nobody offers to beg.' Italics were used to add more emphasis to the loss.[1]

[1] The beauty and simplicity of these sixteenth-century descriptions of dogs is rivalled in a contemporary classic entitled *My Dog Tulip*, life with an Alsatian, by

Charles II was nicknamed 'The King of Curs'—not a particularly flattering title, but much in keeping with those he enjoyed bestowing on others as, for instance, when he made one of his liegemen Governor of Duck Island, or when he made a widow kneel and arise Gentlewoman of the Horse, Lady of the Crupper, Countess of Pall Mall, Viscountess of Piccadilly and Baroness of the Mews. For example, when Béranger came to write his famous history of horsemanship in the next century, he found that, although the practice had long been dropped, a regular charge was made for hempseed to the King's Mews, dating back to the year of the Restoration.

In that same year, a new Mall had been commenced. As it still does today, it ran parallel with Pall Mall. In some plays of the Sixteenth Century, the Mall is referred to as Pall Mall, and vice versa. In telling *The Story of the Pall Mall Gazette*, J. W. Robertson Scott prefaces his first chapter with a note 'for American readers'. 'Pall Mall, pronounced pell mell . . .' begins the note. The confusion has arisen because although the game of pall-mall was first played in the street of Pall Mall, the dust of the coaches and horses made it such that, as soon as the new Mall was laid, the players immediately forsook their old meeting ground for the new one. According to the Oxford Dictionary, *palla* is an Italian variant of *balla* meaning ball; *malleus* is the Latin for hammer—and *pallemaille* (the French alternative), like the English equivalent, means the sport of driving a wooden ball through an iron ring. Croquet is a later offshoot, since in the original game the winner was he who either hit the ball quickest through the ring, or else agreed to do so in a given number of strokes. To fall short either way was to forfeit a round, since victory was awarded on points, and proficient players were proud of their handicaps.

In a book on the *Antiquities of Westminster*, an engraving (but too

J. R. Ackerley (1956). 'Her face also is long and pointed, basically stone-grey but the snout and lower jaw are jet-black. Jet, too, are the rims of her amber eyes, as though heavily mascara'd, and the tiny, mobile eye-brow tufts that are set like accents above them. And in the midst of her forehead is a kind of Indian cast-mark, a black diamond suspended there, like the jewel on the brow of Pegasus in Mantegna's "Parnassus", by a fine dark thread, no more than a pencilled line, which is drawn from it right over her poll midway between the two tall ears. A shadow extends across her forehead from either side of this caste-mark, so that, in certain lights, the diamond looks like the body of a bird with its wings spread, a bird in flight.'

poor to reproduce) shows the King at play in a game that must have been a variation on the traditional form. For a ring is suspended on a pole some twenty feet high and the players appear to be driving at it with mallets. In the background, many of the trees are saplings, so the date must be about 1665. Again, in a bird's eye view of the Park drawn and engraved by Kips in 1712, the game still appears to be a popular pastime.[1]

Spring was always the best season for the game, for then the ground was fresh—as witness Pepys's observations, culled from a ranger, who told him as he swept the Mall that the earth was sprinkled with cockle-shells to keep it fast, but that in dry weather they turned to dust and made the balls go dead. This post was known as 'The King's Cockle-Strewer'.

In 1677, *The Mall or the Modish Lovers*,[2] was first produced. Says the foppish Mr. Lovechange to Mrs. Easy, 'Meet me this night in St. James' Pel Mall.' But it is obvious from her reply that she knew he meant the Park, not the street. The piece was not very successful, and had followed Wycherley's *Love in a Wood* whose success from five years before was still remembered.

Wycherley, so he told Pope, wrote the play at the end of his 'teens. This would have meant the play would have been finished by 1660—although this could not have been the case since in the first act there is both an allusion to gentlemen's periwigs, which only came into fashion in 1663, and to guineas, which were first struck that year; later, there are references both to the vests, which Charles II ordered to be worn in Court in 1666, and to the Great Fire of that year. Probably what he meant was that his first draft was completed by the Restoration.

Lord Macaulay, in an essay on the 'Comic Dramatists' of this period, refers to Spence's *Anecdotes*, in which a tale is told of how driving round 'the Ring' the Duchess of Cleveland (one of Charles II's mistresses) leant out of her coach and bawled at Wycherley: 'Sir, you are a rascal; you are a villain; you are a ——.' This blank, one of

[1] A mell court, badly damaged in the bombing, was reopened in Hampstead in July, 1949, by J. C. Holmes, the American Minister in London. Numbers used in the game on the boarding can be seen in a 1732 print of the Mall (Plate XLIA, facing p. 145).
[2] A play attributed to Dryden.

those infuriating blanks, might have applied as aptly to her own children—at least so speak the vulgarians who have missed the subtlety of Her Grace's powers of repartee. For during the final act of *Love in a Wood*, a song ends:

> Great Wits and great braves
> Have always a Punk to their Mother.

John Dennis, who saw the actual meeting and places it not in 'the Ring', 'but going thro' Pall Mall [i.e. the Mall in this instance] towards St. James's', declares that Her Grace's words were, 'You, Wycherley, you are the son of a Whore', and no sooner had she uttered them than she burst out laughing. At first the dramatist missed the allusion to his song, but suddenly seeing it and remembering that a handsome young lover called Jack Churchill had been rewarded with nearly £5,000 by the Duchess, he shouted to his coachman to turn about, drive back up the Mall, and follow in hot pursuit. As soon as he was alongside her, 'Will *Your Ladyship* be at the play tonight?' he called, doubtless still thinking of her in the heat of the moment as the Countess of Castlemaine which indeed, until eight months before, had been her title. There then followed a dialogue which might have come straight from one of his comedies.

'Will *Your Ladyship* be at the play to-night?' [he repeated].

'Well, what if I am there?'

'Why, then I will be there to wait upon Your Ladyship, tho' I disappoint a very fine woman who has made me an assignation.'

'So you are to disappoint a woman who has favour'd you for one who has not?'

'Yes, if she who has favoured me is the finer of the two. But he who will be constant to Your Ladyship, till he can find a finer Woman, is sure to die your Captive.'

Thus they parted, until the evening—she sitting in the first row of the royal box, he leaning against one of the pillars of the pit in Drury Lane.

In the following spring when the play was printed, a dedicatory letter served as pretext and preface. One passage, superb for its graced expression, has for too long been missed by the anthologists.

I beseech your Grace, have a care for the future; take my counsel, and be (if you can possibly) as proud and ill-natured as other people of quality, since your quiet is so much concerned, and since you have more reason than any to value yourself:—for you have that perfection of beauty (without thinking it so) which others of your sex but think they have; that generosity in your actions which others of your quality have only in their promises; that spirit, wit and judgement, and all other qualifications which fit heroes to command, and would make any but your Grace proud.

How that prose anticipates Newman—though what a strange encounter must it have been when this black sleazy beetle first met the gentle grey grasshopper of a Cardinal!

The actors chosen for the opening performance were a distinguished company. There was Hart, who was only second to Betterton, and played the Ranger; whilst Mohun was cast as Dapperwit, and that 'merry Jade', Mrs. Knipp (who was Pepys's favourite actress) was given the appropriate part of Lady Flippant. Act II, set in the Mall after dark, begins thus:

RANGER: Hang me, if I am not pleased extremely with this new fashioned caterwauling, this midnight carousing in the park.

VINCENT [*a gad about Town*]: A man may come after supper with his three bottles in his head, reel himself sober, without reproof from his mother, aunt, or grave relation.

RANGER: May bring his bashful wench, and not have her put out of countenance by the impudent honest women of the town.

DAPPERWIT: And a man of wit may have the better of the dumb show of well-trimmed vest or fair peruke:—no man's now is whitest.

RANGER: And now no woman's modest or proud; for her blushes are hid, and the rubies on her lips are dyed, and all sleepy and glimmering eyes have lost their attraction.

VINCENT: And now may a man carry a bottle under his arm instead of his hat; and no observing spruce fop will miss the cravat that lies on one's shoulder, or count the pimples on one's face.

DAPPERWIT: And now the brisk repartee ruins the complaisant cringe, or wise grimace.—Something 'twas, we men of virtue always loved the night.

RANGER: O blessed season!

VINCENT: For good-fellows.

RANGER: For lovers.

DAPPERWIT: And for the Muses. . . .

Wycherley's play turned from being the success of the spring season to being the summer talk of the chocolate- and coffee-houses. Lighter

XLII. The Encampment in St. James's Park, 1783; an engraving thought to be by James Fittler.

XLIII. Queen Charlotte Walking in the Park, with a View of Buckingham House;
a coloured print of 1796.

wines were now served at table, wild roses burst in the hedges of Piccadilly, and the heavy scent of limes fell on the sedan-traffic of the Mall. As the end of the century neared, so the Dutch Monarch showed himself as much a lover of bird-life as Charles II. A traveller from Amsterdam writes of a white raven, 'very old and famous', which could be seen as late as 1695 living close to one of the gates leading to Westminster—and in all probability it was the same raven which Pepys mentioned as being purchased just after the Restoration. Moreover, William III built himself a small observation house on Duck Island, to which he would withdraw to smoke his Gouda pipe; it was also 'His Majesty's special command that none presume to keep a fowling piece, gun, setting dog, net, trammel, or other unlawful engine, wherewith to destroy, or kill, or in any way disturb the game . . .'. For already the King had moved his Palace out to Kensington, preferring its quiet lanes with damson trees and gravel pits (so noted for a cure of gout, stitch or gall-stones) to the nightly cries of the piemen or link-boys from the chandlers with their torch flares. In the enchanted Park, exoticism now vied with eroticism; the societies for the propagation of virtue to which the King lent his name failed because, like all such societies whether they be in Leyden or London, the fanatics seized control; and once they had control, the more moderate members, who were prepared to accept human nature for what it was, were soon outnumbered. So all night at the Mulberry Garden loitered wenches, crunching perfumed almonds as they accosted gallants, promising them in turn spiced custards and brandy if they would but call a hackney and visit their rooms in St. Giles. Or at the Chocolate-House, 'The Cocoa Tree' in Pall Mall, the company would sit softening a *damm me* to a more mellifluous *dammé* or *demme*, while in the St. James's Coffee-House, that was so soon to be the favourite lounging place of the Whigs, members would talk of 'jaunting it', by which they meant being a fellow proud to give presents and not count the change.

Here lie the counter-checks to the fictions of historical romance—to the singers with their lutes; the flowing curls of the perfumed periwigs; the gilded sedans moving at the slow pace of a ghostly pavane. For the turn of the century had another side—a *montage* of hot primary colours, with coffee-house signs off Pall Mall marked with stars to denote flagellation, or with men's hands to denote youths for sale; with Bolingbroke, the Secretary of State, laughing at the Queen's Maids of Honour, and bellowing, 'St. James's once housed leprous maidens. Ha, ha. It still does. Ha, ha, ha'; with rips drinking rhenish in the Mulberry Garden, their faces sweating with the pox-pits of wine and women.

Love in a Wood had been given the alternative title of *St. James's Park*—and Wycherley was prophetic. With the Eighteenth Century, eroticism in the Park took the place of exoticism, because exoticism had moved across the water to the Fox Hall Pleasure Gardens. At the same time, these Pleasure and Spring Gardens let the parks once more regain the pastoral quality which they had possessed at the beginning of the Seventeenth Century, since no longer need they provide any amusement other than their ponds, trees and hillocks could afford. 'Delicate walking weather', wrote Swift to Stella in 1711: 'the Canal and Rosamond's Pond full of rabble with skates.' Another fifty years on and the rabble had disappeared, the Serpentine offering a larger and bolder rink. So it was that all through this century St. James's slowly returned to its earlier character of an enchanted forest; a place of sanctuary; and a wood for lovers, stags and kings.

To those pursued by creditors, the Park was accounted 'a verge of the Royal Court' and hence claimed as sanctuary against bailiffs or affidavit-men. In Fielding's *Amelia*, Captain Booth will walk in the Mall when he will not walk elsewhere, and in 1732 an over-earnest Bow Street runner, who made the mistake of trying to serve a warrant near Rosamond's Pond, was imprisoned for his folly.[1]

Nor could a man draw a sword in St. James's. Says Captain Booth, 'My blood rises; I can't stay where he is, and I must not draw in the Park!' So his dilemma becomes threefold; to be thought a coward and

[1] Fielding also tells his readers how all the bawds fled at the approach of Captain Booth striding down the Mall, and in this Fielding was identifying himself with Booth (see p. 174). But not so with James Boswell. Here is a passage from his London journal, dated the 25th March, 1763: 'As I was coming home this night, I felt carnal inclinations racing through my frame. I went to St. James's Park, and, like Sir John Brute, picked up a whore. She who submitted to my lusty embraces was a young Shropshire girl, only seventeen, very well clothed, her name Elizabeth Parker. Poor thing, she had a sad time!' (Sir John Brute is a character who appears in Sir John Vanbrugh's play, *The Provoked Wife*, Act IV, Scene 3.)

not answer an insult, to answer it forthwith and be rushed to a Court of Law, or to answer it beyond the gates and so risk being dashed off to a Court of Bankruptcy. Again, after the failure of the 'Fifteen rising, a soldier was whipped for shouting 'God save King James III', since whipping was within the royal bounds of this sanctuary, just as in the Lord Steward's office of the century before two entries had been lodged, side by side, about two lunatics—one for throwing an orange at the King, the other for throwing a stone at his Queen. Cautious old William III never quite saw the irony of the first missile—though 'he felt its juice' and had the man committed to an asylum. Thus it was stories like these which made Lord Hervey declare England to be the only country where so many clowns were heroes and so many men of quality clowns. Jonathan Swift felt similarly, and at a time when a trip to Town was considered incomplete without a visit to the lions at the Tower, a puppet show, the tombs at the Abbey, the follies of the Mall and the ravings of Bedlam, so it was not surprising that the satirist sometimes turned the order topsy-turvy, juxtaposing the silken fops of the Mall with the coloured calico vests of Mr. Powell's marionettes, or those who roared at the creatures in Bedlam with those that were roared at by the beasts in Lion Tower.

Yet more dangerous than the lions, tigers or catamounts was the roaring Bedlam caused by the Mohawks as they cut their way with tuck, razor and sword through the streets on the borders of the Park. Every time that Swift had his head shaved for the correct sit of his periwig, he would watch the barber nervously; he could never forget the stories of after dark—of faces slashed; carriages overturned; sedans run up to the hilt. 'I walked in the Park this evening, but came home early to avoid Mohawks'—and once home, cracking a walnut for refreshment, the Dean continued with his writing of the 'Argument, proving from History, Reason and Scripture that the present Mohawks and Hawku-bites are the Gog and Magog mentioned in the Revelations.' This was in the year 1712.

For two years these 'bloods' reigned the nightly terror of the Town; if their hooliganism sometimes ended in manslaughter, it was not until public opinion forced the government to offer £100 reward, that four of them were brought to book. But on capture, they reserved their defence, declaring later in Court that they were 'scourers of Mohawks', so, with small fines of a few pence, they were each dismissed—and this dismissal, which was considered by many citizens as an acquittal, was also held as a proof of the corruptions of the period. Many Mohawks were believed to be the sons of Peers and there was thought to be collusion between the judges and the House of Lords.

For a short season, after the Restoration, the Park had been invaded first by Muns, then Hectors, and finally Nickers, whose art it was to break windows with halfpennies; the Hawkubites and Mohawks were in direct descent of this tradition—though their art, if art it can be called, was far more dangerous. With the courage of three bottles in their head, they aimed with rapier or dagger to tattoo the faces of their victims. 'New invented wounds' was how Gay described their feats, and in Steele's *Sir Roger de Coverly* there is a description of a pack pricking a courtier at all angles so that, with his coat tails flying, he is forced to spin like a top. In Number 332 of the *Spectator* they are terms 'Sweaters', because of the way in which they made their victims sweat. In a lesser degree, their mentality is sometimes paralleled by schoolboys when they will stone a weaker of their kind until he dances. Indeed, the forcing of honest wool merchants, tailors and manteau men to act grotesque capers at the point of a sword can perhaps be explained partly as spite motifs for debts incurred and partly as a certain kind of young lord's desire to be revenged on a hard working bourgeoisie. If these terms are borrowed from the psychiatrist's notebook, it is done so knowing that in other words the same truths were observed by Defoe in 1714.

In Close Walk—the Walk running at the head of Rosamond's Pond —the Jacobites and Tories would congregate, referring to the head of the new Hanoverean House as a 'Turnip-boor'. On first awaking in his London Palace, the first of the Georges was reputed to have said: 'The ranger of *my* Park, sent me a fine brace of *my* carp out of *my* canal'; the anti-Whigs seized the phrase, regarding it as something of a tradesman's attitude towards *his* Park, *his* Carp, *his* Canal. When italics failed them, their opposition to this 'offspring of the gingerbread castles of Herrenhausen' took a more open form of insult. The Countess of Darlington and Duchess of Kendal were titles created 'for German

Sultanas' in the opening year of the reign; soon they were known to
the whole Town, because of their shapes, as the 'Elephant' and 'May-
pole' of the Mall. In the last year of the reign, an anonymous author
complained of those in the Mall who thought that they could damn,
drink and dress; who would waddle into church, keep out of debt, and
hum an air from an opera; who could do all these things tolerably—and
yet be only thought well-bred by those in Gracechurch Street. At St.
James's such 'shall not pass muster, but be placed among the "awkward
men", or else be returned like counterfeit guinea[s] that will not go'.

George II was more popular; his tastes if Germanic, were also
sympathetically French; those of the *beau monde* who promenaded
before Marlborough House between the hours of two and twelve and
after seven during the Season began to copy the airs of shepherds and
shepherdesses, wearing aprons, carrying pails, and calling themselves
Corydon and Audrey, Strephon and Delias: but they kept strictly to
the Cockleshell Walk, the Long Lime Walk, which led to the Elm
Grove, or Duke Humphrey's Walk, which was laid out in imitation of
St. Paul's middle aisle. Not for them the following of sheep-tracks to
the meadows of Chelsea, the thymy molehills or mossy eminences of
the Upper Park; and, if pressed to such adventures by their swains
halloo-ing as if to flocks, then the ladies would slightly lift their
hooped skirts, playing for their answer a sort of white satin Bo-peep
with their high heeled shoes; and if pressed again, then with arms
akimbo and ready to spread the path, they would fall back on a line
from Congreve, declaring themselves ready instead 'to laugh at the
great vulgar and the small'.

In their choice lay an artificiality which made them prefer the bulbous
sea-green glass of the print shops to all the waving woodland green of
the Park—since their taste for Arcadia was strictly a stage Arcadia. To
idling hours by the Canal waiting for carp, their lovers preferred the
certainty of trout cooked in marigold leaves in one of the alleys lit by
flambeaux off Old Drury.

If in King James I's reign court life had made pastoral life seem idyllic,
now the pastoral had to be diminished to a quarter strength by the
addition of comical, historical and tragical elements; the gangways of
the playhouses were expected to extend into the open air. Those who

deplored 'the Ring' said that it had served its purpose as had Shakespeare's Globe; those who favoured the Mall found in its sheltering
trees a dome as engaging as Vanbrugh's Opera House in the Hay-
Market, but as accoustically deplorable. 'Lor! How much must a man
shout to make his affairs known to the world.'

The play was the thing. Wycherley's *Love in a Wood or St. James's
Park* had been practically forgotten; in its place in 1773, had come
another piece, borrowing half the same title, and describing itself as
St. James's Park, A Comedy. It was full of pastiche, with Lady Rattle
determined 'to sneer [all the men] out of countenance' and Mrs.
Straddle equally determined 'to jostle all the women'. These were the
clichés of playwriting, and were as dangerous to an Eighteenth Century
dramatist as the phrases 'the beginning of the end' or 'the last analysis'
can be to a modern historian. If Wycherley missed little, there is in this
later play about the Park nothing but the obvious. And yet had there
been the dramatist in the 1730s, what a poetry could have been wrung
out of the cries of the women hawkers in the Park with their lip salves,
night masks and handkerchiefs; their dyes of trotter's oil and bear's
grease to make the dark blonde; their bags of lavender, mouse-skin
eyebrows and twists of saffron.

Queen Caroline put saffron in her tea as a cure for depression.
James I had championed its herbal properties, believing them to cure
eruptive rashes such as measles—a remnant of the old doctrine of
colours—, and in Hanoverian England (as even in 'Lord' George
Sanger's day) it was given to canaries when moulting. Queen Caroline
had enjoyed watching it being administered in the bird shops in St.
Martin's Lane, just as she had enjoyed watching the races from her
Palace window. She had seen a boy circle the ninety-three acres of
St. James's five times in less than two hours; she had seen a calico-
printer from Wandsworth hop a hundred yards of the Mall in forty-
six jumps. (In 1749, a girl of eighteen months crawled it in twenty-three
minutes 'to the great admiration of thousands', said the papers and
doubtless to the great advantage of her parents' purse.) For the Queen
was fonder of watching than walking. One day she had heard cries
for help coming from the direction of Rosamond's Pond (Plate XLIb,
facing p. 145), but mist had prevented her from locating them. Later,

she learned that two sedan carriers had walked into the water by mistake. Thus it was that a railing was put up here, and another round a green in the centre of the Park. (The latter was finally removed in the 1820s.) New gates were erected at Buckingham House and also at the top of Constitution Hill; benches were repainted and the boarding of the Mall for the game of pall-mall renewed. The Whitehall Parade Ground used for drilling troops was paved with stone, though twice in the Eighteenth Century it was flooded by the spring-tides of the Thames.[1] Again, the Queen, followed the precedent set up by Charles II, appointed another Governor of Duck Island in 1735—Stephen Duck, the eccentric poet and thresher.

Duck came from Charlton in Wiltshire, where together with a London servant, he had clubbed together to build a library. That library, collected mostly from second-hand bookstalls, consisted of the Bible and Milton, Seneca's *Morals* and copies of the *London Spy*, some Addison, all Shakespeare, and a good many back numbers of the *Spectator*. When the Queen's appointment was made known to him, he was Keeper of Merlin's cave at Richmond Park; Governor of Duck Island was a decided advancement. He accepted the post readily— but not so readily did he accept the next, a living in Byfleet in Holy Orders. He preferred to be a London poet to an obscure clergyman. The Thames ran through London and in the Thames at Reading, in a fit of melancholy, he drowned himself.

A printer's devil can make a Duck out of a Duke; but the mistake was often made on purpose in the Age of Reason as is obvious from some of the accounts circulated of the Duke of Kingston's party, which was held on Duck Island in the middle of the century.

The Duke of Kingston, the brother of Lady Mary Wortley Montagu, decided to hold an open-air concert, to be followed by a cold collation. Among the guests was the Honourable Miss Chudleigh—in fact, from his point of view, the chief Guest of Honour. She had often been the toast of the Town, her appearance in the Mall fitting the weather to her favourite maxim which was that 'beauty unadorned is beauty most adorned'. Soon, there were two schools of thought about her and each

[1] Many soldiers were drilled and trained here for the American war of Independence; now, every year, it is the scene for Trooping the Colour.

school borrowed a couplet from Pope. The kinder murmured that

> If to her share some female errors fall,
> Look on her face and you'll forget them all,

while the less kind muttered:

> Some men to business, some to pleasure take,
> But every woman is at heart a rake.

Now the facts of the case are that she was Lady in Waiting to the Princess of Wales, that she was married twice (the Duke was eventually a successful suitor), and that for a time she maintained the delicate relationship of being a wife and mistress to two different men. On the summer night of the 7th June, 1751, when she had attended the party on Duck Island, the company were red-faced and had drunk well. Apart from the refreshment which they had brought, many of them had drunk well earlier at *The Vineyard* where sangree, towrow and cyder boiled with Jamaica pepper could be purchased.

This tavern known as *The Vineyard*, and sometimes called *The Royal Vineyard*, stood close to Rosamond's Pond, not far from the old site of James I's Physic and Vine Garden. The tariff included Gripe and Colic Water, Brandy Punch at 2*d*. a quart, Cock Ale and Florence Wine as well as mixtures known as Cuckold's Comfort, Last Shift and Ladies' Delight. Parliament Gin too was sold—an act of defiance against those who had closed the gin shops in the 1730s. For it was against a riot that had broken out to the tune of 'No Gin, No King', that the Grenadier Guards had been called into the Park to quell the mob. They were the first regiment to bivouac there—since at this period soldiers did not sleep in barracks, but were billeted with the inhabitants of Westminster. Hence soldiers frequently committed robberies in the parks and, although on this occasion they did restore order, they failed to prevent the sale of gin. One enterprising chemist in St. James's Market sold bottles, with a prescription advising those suffering from water poisoning to 'take two or three spoonfuls of this four or five times a day, or as often as the fit takes you'. In the streets it was hawked to the cry of, 'Bung your eye! Bung your eye!'

It was after a supper of neats' tongues, goose-pie, sucking-pig and gherkins that the company on Duck Island had sung glees. The place

XLIV. A View of the Horse Guards from Buckingham House; an engraving by H. Schultz, after a drawing by F. I. Mannskirsch, 1813.

XLV. A View of Buckingham House from the Horse Guards; an engraving by H. Schultz, after a drawing by F. I. Mannskirsch, 1813.

evoked memories and soon there were stories of the otter that had taken sanctuary on this very spot, of the hounds that had chased him into the water, of how trying to get to the Canal he had been speared by stalwart Mr. Smith. So well had the otter lived off the fat of the water that he measured five feet, said some; fifteen feet, protested others. But the music had been excellent, the dinner delectable, and the wine superb. Five or fifteen feet—who cared? Fifteen or fifty years— who cared? They would probably all be dead. The Honourable Miss Chudleigh looked at His Grace and realized how much his life was in the full leaf. She thought of what Tasso had said of the rosebud, 'Quanto si mostra men, tanto è più bella'—, and she decided that the poet was wrong.[1]

The Foreigner's Guide of 1752, carried an alternative title that was partly a warning. 'A necessary . . . Companion . . . for the Foreigner and Native', read the second inscription. The word 'Native' is obviously intended with a certain scorn, meaning those not used to the ways of the Town. Although it was not until the last year of the reign, as Walpole observes, that His Majesty paid the nation the compliment of openly taking an English mistress, it was mostly the term 'Frenchified' that was levelled by the satirists at the fashions prevailing in Court circles. Goldsmith's Chinese philosopher finds the ladies of the Mall one day upon stilts, the next upon flat soles. One month their clothes are bloated with whale-bone, the next they are as slim as mermaids. One year it is the hoop which is the mark of distinction in dress, the next it is the train or tail. Whilst Goldsmith was writing, London's Lady Mayoress on days of ceremony was wearing a tail longer than 'a bell-wether of Bantam, whose tail, you know, is trundled along in a wheelbarrow'.

These tails and trains as they blew in and out of fashion have left their mark on the writing of Richardson, Fielding and Smollett. In their descriptions of women it is noticeable how often they break the rule of beginning with the face and begin instead with the shoes, working slowly upwards. Lady Bradshaigh, in a practical joke on Richardson, sent him a note on the publication of the fourth volume of Clarissa, begging him to give the story a happy ending. The novelist in turn

[1] When it reveals itself least, then doth it blow most fair.

begged for a meeting, asking Mrs. Belfour of Devonshire (as Lady Bradshaigh of Haigh had signed herself) to meet him in the Mall. He then goes on to describe himself, adding that he will keep his eyes well to the ground, watching for a pretty foot, and then letting them 'rear up gradually by degrees' to the smile that they anticipate. 'This is very descriptive of the struggle in his character between innate bashfulness and a turn for observation', notes one early editor of the *Letters*.

Yet Richardson does not appear to have suffered from shyness—nor Smollett or Fielding; in fact, Fielding's burly strides had only to be heard crunching over the cockleshells for all the vagrants and loose women to be off. In *Amelia*, the novelist describes his fury at seeing a sentry ill-using a child for trespassing on the King's grass, and he may well have witnessed the scene of the sentry who broke an old man's arm —also for trespassing on the royal verge. There are two sides to a coin, and the golden guineas, stamped with the heads of the reigning Hanoverians, could always be reversed to reveal the yellow haunted faces of the poor. I have heard cowards described by my grandparents as being 'yellow as a guinea', and there is another sense in which the phrase might well have been applied to the London undertide of that age.

No artist saw it better than Hogarth. Watch his line eat into the tarnish and tinselled finery of his characters, or his backgrounds where rouged toffs stand listening to the street-music of beggars, and painted harlots accept the sentimental leave-takings of their protectors in hard cash. In the dimly-lit gutters, children loiter—although it has already struck ten; off Holborn Fields, in Whetstone Park so mocked because its trees were all brick, the only green lies in a rotting cabbage leaf or the shadows used to build up the sickly cheeks of a sneak thief. Or turn towards Rosamond's Pond and watch the caricature of the law forbidding handbags to be carried in St. James's, and the pompous smirks of the three Grenadiers on guard as a ticket-porter carries before him a load of chamber-pots as though they were steaming soup tureens. The dresses on Gainsborough's ladies are like landscapes; they chart the gardens and parks of England. By contrast, in the drawings of Hogarth, the valleys and rivers lie in the wrinkles of the human face; they chart the misery and vanity of the other half of the age.

A priest must keep a strict custody of the eyes; that is a rule of seminary training. It is an admirable precept, but when it is broken it can sometimes lead to some very funny observations, quite different from those of novelists. Poor Padre Batista Angeloni of the Society of Jesus. How the London of the 1750s puzzled him. But how much more puzzled must have been his countrymen when they received this letter:

[Here] the women of quality have much of the shepherdess mien, or rather inclining to something less modest, the nymphs of the town. This air, I presume, these ladies affect for a moral purpose, that by this artifice all kinds of characters in women looking alike, the men shall be afraid to accost any of them, lest peradventure they should meet a virtuous woman, and be rejected with contempt. Thus the dames of avowed pleasure are prevented from exercising all their mischief by being mixed with, and indistinguishable from those of professed virtue, as the same amount of poison diffused through a large quantity of matter is less likely to kill, than in its unmixed state, or wine less apt to intoxicate when it is diffused in water than when taken alone. This policy you must allow to be admirable in favour of virtue and chastity amongst the ladies of England . . .

So it has always been—the two views, the reversible coin. Foreign observation can never be quite the same as home observation; its use must be that of a counter-check—and, between 1750 and 1850 in the Park, check and counter-check must mark the course, each decade of the way.

It has ever been a feature of parks for people to be able to stand and forget time in them. A few minutes' walk from the bustle of the streets and, 'It's hard to believe that you are in a city,' becomes a common sentiment. Disraeli may have expressed the thought more eloquently[1]— but essentially it is in the same tone that Londoners speak today as they did in the Eighteenth Century. Then they would stand on these swards and forget the petitions of the silk weavers, hatters and peru-quiers who had sought their Majesties' increased patronage in the 1760s, forget the arguments and debates over the rights and wrongs of the American War of Independence in the 'Seventies, forget the trickle of exiles that began from France in the 'Eighties and mounted into a torrent during the 'Nineties. Here was sanctuary; here was peace. Heavy spring-tides or a bad flood and once more St. James's became the sea of dark ponds that it had been to the Romans. Yet every time that

[1] See p. 28.

there was such a flooding, more precautions were taken to prevent its recurrence.

A winter hurricane in 1768, followed by ceaseless rain, made cisterns of the basements in Westminster and the need of a February ferry between Storey's Gate and Buckingham House became imperative. The result was that in the late spring it was decided to fill in Rosamond's Pond and the moats around Duck Island: so stagnant were the latter that these channels round the decoy were frequently likened to the canals in Venice. The summer house, which Dutch William had made for himself and to which the Duke of Kingston had invited the Honourable Miss Chudleigh, had come to be known as Webb's House. Webb was the surname of the first Pond Keeper and it is a curious coincidence that he was also flat-footed. But his house had to go—as indeed did Jack.

Jack was a swan. He lived to seventy, killed many dogs, and once nearly drowned a boy who had baited him. Queen Charlotte used to feed him with warm white bread. When the decoy was abolished and he was moved to the Canal, he sailed majestically up and down, attacking any bird that so much as approached him. One day, rather unfairly it seems, a pack of Polish geese, keeping close formation, swam upstream and between them pecked Jack to death. Then the myth began. Stories of his strength were reported and magnified; he was said to be neither a bird nor a beast, neither flesh nor fowl—but a part of the Deity. Some who listened grew sceptical; they said it had been the same story at the death of the Chevalier d'Eon, who was also neither fish nor fowl—or, put more literally, neither man nor woman.

Chevalier Charles Geneviève Louise Auguste André Timothée d'Eon de Beaumont, Knight of the Order of St. Louis, Captain of Dragoons, Aide-de-camp to the Duke de Broglie, Royal Censor of History and Literature, and at one time Ambassador to the Court of St. James's, promenaded regularly between Whitehall and Buckingham House. Despite a strong military career behind him, he was thought to be a woman: bets were placed on his sex, and a gigantic swindle was conceived by a crafty lawyer in Leicester Fields.

In 1770, carriage after carriage arrived, its occupants dismounting hastily, and the lawyer growing richer at the rate of fifteen guineas

XLVI. The Chinese Pagoda and Bridge, 1814; a print published by Whittle & Laurie of Fleet Street to mark 'the Peace Celebration'.

XLVII. 'A Brilliant Suggestion, presented, gratis, to the Horse Guards by Mr. Punch'; a cartoon by John Leech.

every few minutes. If the Chevalier could be proved a woman, he said, these deposits would be multiplied by six; if within ten years no such proof could be substantiated, he would keep the deposits. But perjury had its price. A year later a Lieutenant de Morande swore in Court that his friend was a woman and a doctor was found to testify that the Chevalier suffered from certain female complaints. So now perjury met cunning. The lawyer pleaded in his defence an Act of Parliament that provided that 'no insurance shall be valid where the person insuring cannot prove an antecedent interested in the person or thing insured'. As none of the clients could make such a claim, Lord Mansfield reluctantly accepted the plea. The lawyer remained richer by £75,000. Some contemporaries have believed the Chevalier to be a spy— and hence the origin of the stories about his double sex: they have hinted that it was a subterfuge to focus attention on activities 'other than the primary ones in his life'. At any rate, when he was buried in England, the undertakers had the last word: 'Take him for all in all, he was a man,' they are reported to have said.

In this incident, Lord Mansfield emerges as a strong figure of the English Bench; a few years later, in another incident, he emerges as a typical English romantic.

The Countess de Genlis, who had been a governess to the Duke of Orlean's children, came to England in the early 'Eighties. During her visit, her birthday occurred—a factor Lord Mansfield discovered through a French peerage book. So on the 10th July, he sent her a basket of moss-roses. The Countess was delighted; she had a literary talent—and her thanks were penned in a prose of flowers that attempted to match the gift. When therefore she left for Paris, Lord Mansfield gave her a moss-rose tree, which she in turn gave to Perroy, the famous French nurseryman. So it was that a gift from Caen (Ken) Wood, Hampstead, crossed the Channel for the first time in the Eighteenth Century, has been carefully pruned ever since, and still blooms every summer in the grounds of the Palais Royal.

The next year Madame Roland was a visitor to London. I translate what she wrote to her daughter about the Park.

... Many of the ladies wear lovely white muslin dresses, made exactly like those which we have copied from them, but generally tucked up with *cordons* passing under the skirts, which lift these dresses to just about the height of a petticoat. They all wear caps under their hats—some large, some small. The hat is also very varied in shape, and has ribbons everywhere: yet few of them are so light and elegant as ours. But it is often enough that we wear a certain thing for them to reject it; for, although the vanity of some women makes them rush after our fashions, the general spirit of the nation is to disdain and to affect to avoid them.

This was in 1786. Ten years before, Lady Anna Maria Stanhope had imported from across the Channel a head-dress that consisted of a compact of wool, sheeps' tails, false hair, flowers, gauze, feathers, ribbons, corn, fruit, vegetables and lace; it took three hours to assemble, and its achievement was measured by its height; moreover, once assembled it was maintained for three weeks, a pillow case being used in bed in place of a nightcap. They were known to the London crowd as *Towers of Babel*. When they fell from fashion, nodding plumes took their place; the London crowd now said that should the ladies but drop these feathers a few inches they would sprout wings and be angels. Yet they waited in vain, for within a few months there followed a craze for caps. Some were built like church doors, while others became more elevated—taking for their model the cupola of St. Paul's; then the style fell flat—as flat as a *pancake*, since that was the new style; but soon the pancake rose once again, first into a balloon, then the balloon subsided, and the *cardinal* style came into being. The latter also came from France.

The Dubarry had asked Cardinal Fleury for a present and he had sent her a hat, with the text inscribed, 'Charity covers a multitude of sins'. Determined not to be outdone, she penned her own text on another scrap of paper: 'Charity begins at home'. At Versailles the fashion had flourished; at St. James's it died rapidly. The English Church protested, and the milliners, with aid of scissors, a few pins and extra ribbons, re-christened it the *parachute*. This *parachute*, they told the bishops, would prevent the ladies from tripping. As might be expected, the bishops did not reply—even when the pins fell out. It was left to a German to observe that if after dark the Mall 'shone by the light of an innumerable quantity of lamps', then when 'the sun [shone] the ground sparkle[d] with innumerable pins'.

Such were some of the changing fashions of the last half of the century; in fact, it was argued that the fashions were a distraction from the state of the Park—an excuse offered by Lord Offord on more than one occasion.

For a quarter of a century, Lord Offord had remained unmoved by petitions or letters, newspaper complaints or sets of verses.

> Deck anew the flow'ry sylvan palaces,
> And crown the forest with immortal graces,

sang one ballad-monger: and another,

> Make James's Park in lofty numbers rise
> And lift her Palaces unto the skies.

Thunder and lightning, however, cannot be ignored—and the improvements caused by the winter storm of 1768 have already been mentioned; three months later followed another storm, more violent than the first, and causing further improvements. This time a subterranean drain burst and trees were uprooted—one oak falling across the opened sewage channel and so swamping the ground. George Selwyn was now provoked to likening the Park to the Civil List: both were drains on the national economy, and Lord Offord, while tending to agree, had his own modifications to add. In his opinion, the Park was useful grazing land for deer and cattle. His views had always been strictly utilitarian, and from the cattle and the Milk Fair held near the Whitehall boundary there was a regular revenue to be drawn. He was not a romantic and did not care for history; he could not care less if somebody called Tom Brown had made immortal the Seventeenth Century cry of, 'A can of milk, fair ladies.' To him the continued cry of these butterwomen merely meant grazing dues, and it was this financial motive that also preserved the Milk Fair through the larger part of the Nineteenth Century.

Again, it was a utilitarian view of this royal acreage that led Lord Offord to suggest to the King that he might quarter an army here during the Gordon Riots 'or subsequent uprisings' (Plate XLII, facing p. 164). Thus might Parliament and the Crown be protected in the case of an emergency, and the expenses incurred be halved. So in June, 1780, four thousand troops were ordered to strike camp. On the first night, neither tents nor straw were forthcoming. The King spent until dawn encouraging his men as he walked up and down amongst them.

'A little touch of Harry in the night' is about the most embarrassing line in any leading actor's repertoire, and many a scribbler for the *St. James's Chronicle* may well have smiled when, remembering his Sovereign's dictum that Shakespeare wrote much sad stuff, he saw this portly figure talking with the soldiers. Perhaps a comparison between 'this round Hanoverian and the fiery King at Agincourt' has about it something of the slick journalist or undergraduate—and perhaps it may well have been some such thought which prompted an Oxford student to continue:

Although all scenery except the scenery of the playhouse was lost upon me, I have thought since of the picturesque view St. James's . . . then presented. The encampment which had been formed there in consequence of the recent riots, was breaking up; but many tents remained, seeming to be scattered, from the removal of others out of the formal line which they originally exhibited. The effect they produced under the trees and near the canal was commonly gay and pleasing.

These *Random Records* of George Colman, covering more than fifty years, were published in the 1830s. They bridge a gap that includes the completion of the American Civil War of Independence, the end of the French Revolution, and the defeat of Napoleon. As far as the Park is concerned, they bridge the closing stages of Whig grandeur and the beginnings of staid respectability. Between the two lies the Regency and, significantly enough, that bridge over the Canal with its oriental pattern (so fitting to the willows), which elicited from Canova the comment: 'It is strange that this trumpery Chinese bridge should be the production of a government, whilst that of Waterloo was the work of a private company.'

Larwood laughed Canova out of court for his judgment. In this, he is a typical child of the late Victorian Age. In the beginning of the new century, before the Canal had been transformed into a Lake, it was known as the Ornamental Water; in contrast, the Thames was regarded as a riverway of commerce. The difference is revealing, hinting if even indirectly at the industrial revolution to come in trade and all forms of commerce. Again, with secession of America from the mother country and the Restoration of the Bourbons, parliamentary oratory began slowly to decline. In the coalition government, the pointed and rounded periods had reached their peak as an art; then they over-reached, became top-heavily Gothic, and something more functional was demanded. Burke's and Fox's orations, which have the perfection of sonnets, were regarded as better not imitated, better left with other sonnets—on the unread shelves of country house libraries. Rhetoric had led to the excesses of bombast and the excesses of bombast in turn had led to a boring but utilitarian austerity. As always, there were brilliant exceptions like Cobden and Disraeli, or Asquith and Churchill who, both within living memory, have called members to order on points of grammar. And what a superb respect for language that showed—although what had already become a movement in decline when 'the Blenheim Pup' (to quote the *Pall Mall Gazette*) had first entered the House at the end of the century had been merely a trend ninety years before. Moreover, as the Nineteenth Century progressed, so the Commons passed more and more bills enclosing the greens and commons of England; at times, even the royal parks were threatened—there being mooted at one time the building of a Houses of Parliament in Green Park and the building of a new Royal Palace in Hyde Park. So it was that the greens and commons which had once been famous for their highway robberies were now in turn robbed of their freedom and sold into private hands—or at least such might well have been the arguments of a Radical speaker in the 1830s. In St. James's, what had begun as fancy dress—Regency top-hats and trousers—became the accepted fashion in place of knee-breeches and wigs; the dress remained, but the fancy passed away from the Mall.

The picture that *Random Records* suggests is one of continuous *montage*—revolt against conformity, but conformity staying and revolt growing to be regarded more and more as eccentricity; and eccentricity, of course, can be easily dismissed. It is never dangerous because it is never more than the cult of the few. As an old man George Colman heard speeches, rallying volunteers with cries that hearts of oak were needed; the names of Nelson and Wellington were bandied about, recalling for him the ships of the line made of the

stoutest timber for Trafalgar and the butts made from trees for
the rifles used in the famous 'squares' formation at Waterloo. Like the
Elizabethan Latin inscription near Storey's Gate, he remembered that
the Army's strength lay in the Fleet; sea-power, as it had been since the
Roman and Norman invasions or with the Armada or defeat of the
Continental Blockade, was always the decisive factor. Yet as he mused
he began to think that the oak that had furnished the universities with
its stout beams, that brought the port wine to life on the refectory
tables in Hall, was in danger of being forgotten; he remembered his
own College, where Latin had been almost his second tongue. In-
dustrialism was changing the England in which he had grown up;
now, in old age, even the idea of a classical education was being
undermined. In a century, he prophesied, the cavity would show. Vast
changes had taken place since he had walked in St. James's as a young
man, looking at the tents pitched by the Canal. Things had been
shaped anew, like that Canal.

One August Bank Holiday I remember picking up a brochure in
the Park that had been issued by a Careers firm, slanted towards
Classical students leaving the Universities. Latin, it said, was still of use
to those pursuing the Law or Medicine. Latin, it went on, was useful
even in a Ministry—or for entering the Church. Nothing was mentioned of entry to the Church through baptism, and I remember thinking that summer's day of the imprecision of thought and language in
such a brochure. Now when I write the last chapter of this volume, the
word *useful* looms large. The Nineteenth Century was the beginning
of a utilitarian era—and as early as 1814 the beginnings were there.
Nash was asked to help with the peace festivities; the Committee
thought a Pagoda on the Chinese Bridge would be useful. As he began
to think of his work in terms of decoration, so meanwhile the Committee began to weigh up a profit and loss account. After two hours,
they were unanimous in their decision that an entrance fee of half a
guinea would be both a fair and *strategic* sum on the appointed night.

Timed with the miniature naval celebrations on the Serpentine
and the Temple of Concord in Green Park, were the celebrations of St.
James's. Yet whereas entrance to the first two were free, in the case of
the latter barricades were erected and toll gates set up. The plan, in the

minds of the Committee, had been that after a certain amount of free entertainment, the desire for more would spread and a steady stream of people would make their way through Hyde and Green Parks to St. James's. This was precisely what happened—but it happened in such a flood that the gates had to be closed. St. James's was filled to capacity to witness the chief attraction, Nash's Pagoda—an attraction somewhat in keeping with the fairs being then held both in St. James's and in Hyde Park.

All the lawns on both sides of the Ornamental Water were decorated with stars and lanterns, while in the centre, crowning all, blazed a beacon of fire. (Nash may well have studied the Temple of Peace of 1749 and hoped to succeed where Servandoni's plans had failed: for in Green Park Servandoni had crowned his Temple with a pole supporting what he intended should be a monstrance of fire that would turn the night into day.) Certainly, the effect in St. James's was dazzling (Plate XLVI, facing p. 176).

Gaslight was used and small flames in lamps burnt before reflectors; these reflectors were silver lustre and their purpose—not too successful —was to relieve the glare and bring harmony to the whole conception. But in fact, so bright was the achievement (gas was still a novelty) that many spectators could only glance momentarily and then turn away towards the flagpoles supporting the Chinese lanterns, or the trees swathed in spirals of artificial starlight. At ten the firework display began. Inside the Pagoda, rockets, *pots de brin* and roman candles were let off and all was well, until suddenly the top three storeys of the tower caught alight. One workman jumped and cracked his skull on a floating raft in the Canal; another ran out of the building, but died shortly afterwards of severe burns. The Fire Brigade were unable to control the situation and the next morning all that remained was a bridge with the stump of a pagoda on it. Four years later, a Manchester cotton merchant after crossing it—always a tricky task because the hooks to which the catherine wheels had been attached were still left in the timber—expressed considerable contempt for those who had so extravagantly 'thrown away public money'.

The half-burnt bridge brought an air of desolation to the Park— a desolation only further increased by the fair which had been held close to it. When the booths were removed, parts of the turf had been worn a sombre brown; when the marquees for baked meats were folded away, patches of grass were seen to have been singed black. On the banks of the Canal, slime had gathered, and on the open spacious lawns the pits used as ovens were left to gape emptily. The paint from the benches had blistered, the fencing been scorched. The landscape was shabby and scarred—in fact, at six hundred years' remove, it was as if the leprosy housed in the Hospice of St. James had become active again and this time spread to the surroundings.

It was not, however, until the 19th January, 1827, that a Treasury minute agreed that the condition of the Park should be remedied. To this end, for the second time, Nash was called in. Now Nash who was born in the same year as the landscape gardener Repton and who at times had collaborated with him, had no love of symmetry. A view of St. James's from Buckingham House (then converting into Buckingham Palace) revealed a design somewhat like a kite, with the Canal running through it as the main strut. And if the image of the kite is accepted, then it must be added that after the bleak Christmas of 1836 it was a singularly tattered and weather-beaten kite. So one of Nash's first aims was to break down the symmetry. He began by ordering work-men to dig the Canal into a Lake, sink islands at each end—the eastern one of which immediately became known as a new Duck Island—and throw a new bridge[1] across the water.

The Mall was widened—though it never reached the width for quadruple traffic which is what he had in mind, nor were the three terraces to the north built: instead, in their place, were two—Carlton House Terrace East and West. The three terraces to flank Birdcage Walk were begun, the old houses remaining and Wellington Barracks being added. The pot-holes and pits were filled in, and Nash, whose royal patron all along had been the Prince Regent, supervised the planting of trees, bushes and shrubs. Iron railings replaced the decayed

[1] This proved only temporary. A second bridge went up in 1857, condemned a century later—and a new bridge, designed by Eric Bedford, has now replaced it. The disadvantage of Rendell's bridge decorated by Wyatt was that for all ceremonial and royal occasions it had to be propped up from beneath, and the sum needed for annual repairs surpassed the sum bequeathed by an anonymous donor for a new bridge and its general maintenance. Bedford's bridge was therefore opened to the public on 5th October, 1957.

XLVIII. The Cottage erected on Duck Island for the Ornithological Society of London; a drawing made on stone by the architect, I. B. Watson, 1841.

XLIX. 'The St. James Fashions of the 1850's'; from a coloured print drawn and engraved by T. C. Graff.

and burnt wooden fencing. There has been little alteration since—
save for the addition of some statuary, a refreshment kiosk (referred to
as 'The Cake House' on maps), and a few lodges for keepers.

When trousers were first introduced in the Mall (Plate XLIX,
facing p. 185), they were thought to be slightly oriental—just as for
over a century St. James's has always been thought to be London's
most oriental park. These narrow cylinders of fashion, worn by the
Regency bucks, became associated in the practical business mind with
the extravagances of the Brighton Pavilion, or the florid language of
Byron. Byron is perhaps as much the poet of this Park as Chopin is its
musician. 'I realized how much Lady Byron must have bored him'
—and immediately there was, as it were, an invisible linking
between this white, frail spirit and the dashing poet who was the hero
of the *Childe Harold*.

The year was 1848, when Revolution had whisked this Polish
émigré across the Channel. To his apartments in Dover Street came
Vardot and Dickens, Mario and Carlyle to pay homage; bowls of
violets stood on the three pianos in his sitting room—an Erard, a
Pleyel, and a Broadwood delivered by kind Mr. Broadwood himself.
Soon there were intimate recitals in Carlton Terrace and at the home of
the Countess of Jersey in St. James's Square; there was patronage
from their Graces of Westminster, Somerset and Sutherland;
and—so unpleasant but necessary—there was the whisper of Madame
Rothschild to advise what fees to ask. In Lancaster House a thousand
lustres tinkled and vibrated to his crescendo. And beneath that ceiling
of crystal, lost in the reverie of a nocturne, he saw the image of a
thousand castles rise in the glow of a thousand candles. Fact and fancy
leapt together in the brilliance of the occasion—just, as one morning
later, he peopled Nash's polygon room, with its squares chalked for
twelve sets of dancers, its eight glass walls draped with muslin, and its
umbrella roof decorated with gilt cord. He had made the journey out to
Woolwich to see 'this temple of a tent', which had stood temporarily
in the Palace garden of Carlton House for the celebrations of the 1814
Treaty of Paris. Here, south of the river, he had found the elegance of
line and note of interrogation which his own music sought; here, in his
imagination, he had seen again the triumphs of aristocracy—as he had

N

known them in Warsaw and he was ever to remember them one London evening in the June of the past Season. As Chopin made his way back over Westminster Bridge, he dismounted from his carriage at Whitehall. Through the Park, cutting by the narrows, he made his way slowly towards Dover Street. In an alley, he heard a beggar begin to play some musical glasses; the notes eddied, piercing his soul like some siren song. This was also the city of child labour, child prostitution —a city at times hardly fit for children. Mudlarks scavenged the Thames for coal at a farthing a bucket. An order in Wellington Barracks still informed Gentlemen of the Guards that umbrellas might be carried in the purlieus of St. James's—though in the field it would not only be ridiculous but unmilitary. Every day the horse-drawn traffic in the Mall increased: the century was approaching its halfway mark. As Dr. Edward Henry Manning crouched close to the spluttering lamp fitted in his phaeton so that he might lose no time for reading, so Prince Albert relaxed, his back responding to the prim solidity of a Victorian nursery chair, as the laughter of the halls resounded and he caught their echo in those other halls now planned for his Great Exhibition and the beginning of the Crystal Palace era.

Moby Dick was published in America during the year of the Great Exhibition. A passage in it recalls Melville's visit to the capital in the 1840s, where John Murray was his first publisher of *Typee*. He writes of Nelson, standing on a capstan of gun metal, on the masthead of a ninety-nine foot granite column in Trafalgar Square. He continues: '... even when most obscured by the London smoke, token is yet given that a hidden hero is there; for where there is smoke, there must be fire'.

This saying, so paradoxical and yet tipped with that lunatic quality which is so often the mark of genius, represents imaginative writing at its best. But in the last half-century, with the invention of wireless, another view has been revealed which still awaits imaginative photography at its best. Stand in the centre of the Horse Guards Parade and move back towards the Prime Minister's garden: above the Admiralty roof, with its conning towers that can control any part of the Fleet, rises a complicated nest of wire-work; into this crow's nest, as it were, Nelson suddenly looms into view—or step a few yards further back and he appears to be standing amid all the ropes and coils of a modern harbour.

Other heroes of this Park include Captain Cook in the Mall (1914), Lord Clive, facing the Lake from the steps leading up to King Charles Street (1916),[1] and Lord Kitchener who keeps watch from the back of the Prime Minister's house (1926). Cook holds a telescope and Clive a sword, whereas Kitchener merely has his arms crossed. It is noticeable that the statuary of heroes is becoming less belligerent. Again, there is a tendency—more noticeable in St. James's than either Hyde Park or Kensington Gardens—for statuary to become symbolic and, as it becomes symbolic, so it commemorates acts of common endeavour rather than the achievement of one particular sailor or soldier. For instance, in the Mall, Adrian Jones's Royal Marine Memorial for the South African War is a simple bronze relief of the marines storming a kopje and repelling an attack at Peking, and, in the Horse Guards Parade, Gilbert Ledward's five bronze guardsmen, commemorating the Great War, stand before a plain cenotaph.

Two curious 'monsters' of the Horse Guards Parade are a Turkish gun and a French mortar of Napoleon. The gun bears the date 1524, was captured in 1801, and placed in its present position in 1814. An inscription reads: 'The Solomon of the Age, the great Sultan commanded [this] dragon himself to be made. When [it] breathe[s], roaring like thunder, may the enemy's forts be razed to the ground.' The barrel rests on a sphinx, the wheels of its carriage are hubbed with the faces of lions, and there are panels both of a man-eating alligator and of Britannia sitting with a lion looking towards the Pyramids. The same birthright of dragonhood is suggested in the mortar, cast for the Peninsular Campaign. Resting at an angle of 45°, its barrel is supported by the head of a griffin, whose scaly body as it uncoils splits into two small, but no less terrifying heads. It is said to have lobbed shells up to 108 lbs at the Alameda. Myself, I think that the allusion intended must be to the three-headed, three-bodied monster King Geryon whom Hercules defeated. This ornamental support is said to have originated from Woolwich—an 1818 afterthought. Doubtless this

---

[1] This statue was first set in the gardens of Gwydyr House, Whitehall, in 1912, but removed to its present site in 1952.

would explain its mount, with its literal and symbolic twist in the dragon's tail.

At the New Admiralty Arch, designed by Sir Aston Webb, Gunnery and Navigation are celebrated in the form of cherubs.[1] They smile ironically—and war has a different face, almost a pacifist face. Nearby stands the figure of James II, sculptured by Grinling Gibbons; he is crowned with a laurel wreath, holds an outstretched scroll, and is wearing sandals whose laces overlap at the calves where they are fastened by clasps in the shape of lions' heads. The same motif recurs on the tunic. Further down, beyond the Duke of York's Steps, is the recent statue erected to George VI. Then at the far end of the Mall, dead centre and lost in the traffic, rises the 2300 ton carrara marble island that is the Queen Victoria Memorial. Around their thirteen foot high Sovereign[2] are the figures of Victory, Courage and Constancy; Justice (on the north), Truth (South) and Motherhood (west). The work is that of Sir Thomas Brock, who watched his monument unveiled by King George V in the presence of the last German Emperor in 1911.

Around this Memorial, forty thousand tulips are planted each year (the bulb nurseries are in Hyde Park); these are followed by fourteen thousand geraniums (also kept under glass for their winter hibernation in Hyde Park). In charge of these flower beds is the Park Superintendent, who with a team of three hundred and seventy-five workers is responsible, too, for the cutting of the grass on the roof of the Admiralty Citadel. The latter was erected during the second World War; during the first, the Lake was dredged and extra canteens and bungalows were erected to house and feed additional staff from the War Office. (This feat was made easier, since Nash's transformation of the Canal into an Ornamental Water had necessitated the raising of the original bed, so that nowhere was there a depth of more than four feet.) Moreover in each case, during both wars, the War Office was assisted by the Office of Works, under whose management the Parks were placed through an Act of Parliament by the Crown in 1851.

[1] It was erected in 1910 as part of a national memorial to Queen Victoria. In the rooms above the arches is housed the Royal Naval Library.

[2] See p. 30. Often the heights of royal statuary emphasize curious ironies!

In peace time, the rangers work in the closest co-operation with the police. I mention this here, because every spring the word goes from seedsman to under-gardener, from gardener to keeper, that a family of mallards are nesting in the tulips around the Victoria Memorial. The message is then passed on to the police. For before the spring is out, the mallards are on the march. Led by the elder ducks, the younger follow—all the way up Constitution Hill, across Hyde Park Corner (where the traffic is held up), and on until they reach the Serpentine. This is one of the most curious sights of the year—possibly paralleled by the sight of the Balearian crane with the wooden leg, seen by Evelyn in 1664.

Evelyn had noted as well how he had examined the throat of an *Onocrotylus* 'or pelican, a fowl between a stork and a swan', which had been the gift of the Russian Ambassador in Astrakhan. At the moment, there are two pelicans, an Eastern White and an American White— both gifts, one from the Amir of Bahawalpur, the other from the Governor of Louisiana. They are fed at three during winter afternoons, at four in the summer. In either case, it is quite a ceremony since people gather for it as they do for the same sight in Regent's Park Zoo; and in St. James's Park, Duck Island represents a kind of miniature bird zoo.[1] There are many species of waterfowl—among them geese, swans, pochard, teal, wigeon, mandarin and South African shelducks—and there are cormorants too: these were brought from the Megstone Rock off the Outer Farnes in 1888. More recently 'ringing' has taken place, and gulls seen over the Park have later been reported seen in Germany and the Scandinavian countries. So the traditions begun by Charles II are being both developed and sustained.

For the attraction of this 'strip of river', 'sheet of Canal' or 'Eastern Lake' is that it has always offered a waterfront. Over the hills and far away, over the water and far away—here spring immortal longings; a desire for the *ultima thule*, or haven after a rough passage. In St. James's Forest, Fields, Farm and Park, there have ever been watchers— the eye of bird, beast, man and camera: in that order they were

---

[1] On it the Ornithological Society have a Lodge, designed by J. B. Watson. It has stood for over a century, but for some years it has lain under the threat of demolition (Plate XLVIII, facing p. 184).

created and in that order they have come. Once the upper branches of the tall trees swayed to the savage lunge of a wounded bear, and would suddenly flutter with wings: then there would be momentary silence, the crack of brushwood, and the hunter with his spear would close in for the kill. Later, whisps of smoke above the tangle of green would signify a Roman sacrifice being offered at the Temple of Apollo; on the same site, later still, smoke was a sign that the monks were celebrating a feast on their island at Westminster. The Saxon diet of wild bear and wild berry increased to include fish from the river, water fowls from the ponds, and meat from the farm.

'Wood biting bears' or 'wode biting beares': both versions appear in *The Cloud of Unknowing*, but the spelling of the anonymous Fourteenth Century author tells its own tale of the wild life in the London forests. For as the scene changes, and one age merges into another, so the smoke issuing from the village at Charing becomes one year a mighty bonfire as flames burst the barriers of the old gabled City in 1666. The forest has been cleared and the pools drained; now the skyline closes in and the Fields that have made a Farm into a Park are bounded with walls. All around, red brick and white steeples mark three horizons; then slowly that brick mellows and the new brick used is of a browner order. With the Regency, yellow stucco sweeps along the half mile of Mall, while Queen Anne architecture still reigns to the south: from the east blows the smoke of industry, ready to impose its dull ivy over the Horse Guards, the Admiralty and the War Office. The green of the Park merges into the grey of the City.

As omnibuses take the place of horse-drawn coaches and as trams slowly give way to the superior speed of electric trains, so the dormitories of London are spread further and further away from the central hub of government; yet in distance measured by time, they are being brought closer every year. The M.P. of fifty years ago who thought nothing of an hour's walk and whose constant practice of the habit has cheated rheumatism, may well find now that when he is leaving home, another member is just leaving St. Albans or Brighton. For if a franchise were taken of Westminster and Whitehall, it would show that a resident population living within two miles of the area is less than a thirteenth of its daily working population. Yet if as the city has expanded, workers have looked both more and more towards the country for their hours of rest and towards the rural walks of the parks for their lunch-hours, then many of the same delights as of a century ago have remained.

In Whitehall, clerks still gaze from their desks as a troop of Life Guards swing from the Mall towards Storey's Gate, their plumes dipping, their breastplates gleaming. This is the first sign of the military advance of spring—a preparation for the Sovereign's Official Birthday. And each time, there are as many crowds on the gravel paths to watch the rehearsals as there are in stands to watch the event; in anticipated repetition lies the sought-for pleasure. For the scene is re-enacted with a splendour reaching back through countless reigns. Yet across the water, in Boston or Philadelphia, tourists have sometimes been questioned as to whether their formal snapshots were not copies of the coloured prints of another age.

Cecil Rhodes was the first statesman 'to become colour-blind between the British Empire and the American Republic'. This was said of him by one of his biographers, W. T. Stead—an editor of the *Pall Mall Gazette*, whose offices lay a few hundred yards from the Park. Yet to recall Stead's editorship is inevitably to recall the first editor, John Morley. 'I have scribbled many a day on an empty paunch.' The cry links up with those Eighteenth Century 'scribblers' observed by Goldsmith whose fortunes in St. James's were such that they need must walk rather to forget than remember their appetites. Yet, with the increase in printing, more and more of these so-called 'scribblers' of the Nineteenth and Twentieth Centuries not only made good, but within twenty years became creators of public opinion. They were the writers and poets, whose aptitude for political and literary journalism, makes Carlyle's question particularly pertinent: 'Is not every editor a ruler, being a persuader?' Certainly many of them grew editorially powerful —though perhaps, better than answering Carlyle thus, it were wiser to amplify his statement with one from a poet—namely, Yeats:

> Better go down upon your marrow bones,
> And scrub a kitchen pavement, or break stones
> Like an old pauper, in all kinds of weather;
> For to articulate sweet sounds together

Is to work harder than all these, and yet
Be thought an idler by the noisy set
Of bankers, schoolmasters, and clergymen
The martyrs call the world.

Like the writers of any generation, whether their medium was prose or poetry, drama or straight reporting, they all proved themselves unacknowledged legislators—but particularly social legislators: they had a natural sympathy with the underdog because they had nearly all known that position themselves. In the long view, to be born in the first decade of Queen Victoria's reign or the last made little difference. If they had not witnessed child labour or child prostitution themselves, at least they had heard all about it direct from their elders: they were united in their protest. Sir Compton Mackenzie has written of his early Oxford days, when at the beginning of each vacation, the undergraduates would take cabs at Paddington Station, adding that it was their custom to hire boys to carry their luggage, put it in their cabs, and then follow at the run 'until the destination for its unpacking had been reached'. The reward was usually sixpence; the result, more often than not, weak lungs and a premature death. Those who wrote to abolish these evils were sometimes journalists, and sometimes journalists who were also authors. To be an author and a journalist was still an honourable joint-profession, since the latter profession had not yet been abused. Naturally the payments for these services were often negligible. Reviewers of the *Pall Mall Gazette* were expected either to keep the books which were sent to them as their own reward, or else return them and receive a fee; and this was a practice maintained from the beginning unto its last editorship under the late Donald M. Sutherland.[1]

I mentioned earlier Stead's admiration (inherited from his father) for Rhodes as 'the first statesman to grasp the sublime conception of the essential unity of [the English and American] races'; and I mentioned at the beginning of this chapter, as a personal reflection drawn from walking down the Mall, how much was to be learnt from the way that Chinese or Dutch people could emigrate to the United States and within a few months become one hundred per cent American in their new allegiances. Perhaps a United Nations Force attempts to imitate a

[1] This fact was told me by my father, who served on the *P.M.G.*

192

similar achievement. For never before was the world so on view to the newspapers; no action of any consequence can be carried out without the Press hounds catching wind of it and closing in. By and large, I think that this, more than anything else, will come to prove itself one of the major deterrents to acts of aggression and gangsterism. The effect will not be immediate nor do I wish to claim that there will be no more such acts. As in the past, they will be perpetrated—but they will be known for what they are; and tyranny can only change its name when a whole world is subject to it.

This is a parenthesis of global implications, and it is introduced at the end of a book largely concerned with London topography, because perhaps it has a special relevance here.

At coronations or jubilees, at royal marriages or national celebrations, immense crowds gather at the gates of Buckingham Palace, shouting for the Sovereign. Through the loud speakers fixed in the trees, massed military bands play, punctuated by recordings of 'Land of Hope and Glory'. There was a time when the bombast of the words counted:

> God Who made thee Mighty, make thee Mightier yet.

That has changed, the words have become subsidiary to Elgar's stirring music. The accent, if there is an accent, is on the 'Mother of the Free'; and by 'Free' is not meant a pass for licence, but liberty, a liberty in which each man has his own unique voice and his own appointed place. Moreover I say 'accent', for this is a striving, not an accomplished fact. In human terms, whereas a perfect society is an impossibility, a healthy one is not. For all the time—and this is as true as when Morley first noted it: 'principles and aims are coming into prominence which would hardly have found a hearing twenty years ago'.

The human spirit is like grass; it can be trampled, but it rises again; green is the colour of resurrection. Everywhere nature offers such parables. Bees and ants, caterpillars and butterflies: the first wear out their lives for their community—yet 'he that loses his life shall find it'; in the second, according to Christian theology, life is like a caterpillar through which man must pass to death, the chrysalis from which his soul will soar. Yet here, too, there is a duality: in Westphalia the butterfly is a symbol of evil, whereas in Moravia the hunter puts it in his gun to inspire a true aim; in Essex, local inhabitants nip off the head of the first white to bring them luck, whereas in the Cameroons the native shuns the brown species as a God of Revenge; in the Slav countries at a death, the windows are opened to let the spirit depart, whereas two hundred years ago in St. James's, John Gay in deadly solemnity declared that 'they were at best . . . but a caterpillar, drest'. These, then, are some of the stories picked up from conversation and folklore. Myself, standing near the Cockpit Steps off Birdcage Walk, I have seen red admirals, peacocks, painted ladies and meadow browns —just as I have watched old men and boys with their nets making their way towards these flower beds. Both come early, but the men stay longer; they are less agile than they were. Some of them can remember eighty years ago when St. James's was called a Park of Green Palaces; to others, of no particular address or time, it has always served them as a great green hospital. History is brought here by word of mouth, their voices coming in one after another, as with the mediaeval chroniclers. Yet, like those before them, their walks of life are as different as the walks by which they have come; and when dusk falls—surrounded by the towers, cupolas and spires of Piccadilly, Whitehall and Westminster—their vagrant figures dissolve like shadows in the vast descending dark of London Green.

January 1956–January 1959

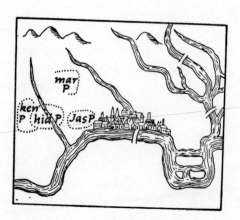

SELECT BIBLIOGRAPHY

General

John Stow: *Survey of London* (1598)

John Stow: *Survey of London,* 'corrected, improved and very much enlarged by John Strype' (1720)

Thomas Allen: *The History and Antiquities of London* (1827-8)

Henry Mayhew: *London Labour and the Poor* (1851)

John Timbs: *Curiosities of London* (1867)

Edward Walford: *London Old and New* (1878)

Jacob Larwood: *The Story of the London Parks* (1881)

Walter Besant: *Survey of London* (1902-12)

J. J. Sexby: *Municipal Parks and Gardens of London* (1905)

G. Head: *The Buried Rivers of London* (1907)

E. Cecil: *London Parks and Gardens* (1907)

A. S. Foord: *Springs, Streams and Spas of London* (1910)

Mortimer Wheeler: *London in Roman Times* (1930)

William Kent: *An Encyclopaedia of London* (1937)

R. S. R. Fitter: *London's Natural History* (1945)

John Summerson: *Georgian London* (1945)

London Museum Catalogue: *London in Roman Times* (1946)

Nikolaus Pevsner: *London: Except the Cities of London and Westminster* (1952)

Neville Braybrooke: *This is London* (1953)

Richard Church: *The Royal Parks of London* (1956)

Nikolaus Pevsner: *London: The Cities of London and Westminster* (1957)

F. R. Banks: *The Penguin Guide to London* (1958)

M. D. R. Leys and R. J. Mitchell: *A History of London Life* (1958)

Kensington Gardens

Lytton Strachey: *Queen Victoria* (1921)

195

W. H. Hudson: *Birds in London* (1898)

Ezra Pound: *Selected Poems* (1948)

James Barrie: *Peter Pan in Kensington Gardens* (1906)

W. B. Yeats: *Reveries over Childhood and Youth* (1915)

W. N. P. Barbellion: *The Journal of a Disappointed Man* (1919)

Christina Rossetti: *Poems* (1891)

Wilfrid Rooke Ley: *Promenade* (1932)

Wyndham Lewis: *Blasting and Bombadiering* (1937)

Wyndham Lewis: *Rude Assignment* (1947)

Ronald W. Clarke: *The Royal Albert Hall* (1958)

Anthony Steele: *Jorrock's England* (1932)

Humbert Wolfe: *Kensington Gardens in War-Time* (1942)

Helen Roeder: *Saints and their Attributes* (1955)

W. S. Scott: *Green Retreats* (1956)

Wallace Stevens: *Selected Poems* (1953)

Augustus J. C. Hare: *Walks in London* (1878)

William Gaunt: *Kensington* (1958)

Hyde Park

R. A. Knox: *Enthusiasm* (1950)

George Orwell: *Down and Out in Paris and London* (1933)

The Puffin Song Book of the Last Sixty Years (1956)

E. I. Watkin: *Poets and Mystics* (1952)

W. Graham Robertson: *Time Was* (1931)

George Clinch: *Mayfair and Belgravia* (1892)

Henry Gibbs: *Theatre Tapestry* (1952)

Lytton Strachey: *Eminent Victorians* (1918)

John Ashton: *Hyde Park* (1896)

E. Dancy: *Hyde Park* (1937)

Bonar Thompson: *A Hyde Park Orator* (1934)

H. J. Massingham: *London Scene* (1934)

W. H. Hudson: *Green Mansions* (1904)

H. V. Morton: *A London Year* (1926)

B. G. Bompas: *A Life of Frank Buckland* (1885)

SELECT BIBLIOGRAPHY

Green Park

David Cecil: *The Young Melbourne* (1939)
Muriel Jaeger: *Before Victoria* (1956)
Hubert van Zeller: *Family Case-Book* (1950)
C. H. Gibbs-Smith: *Balloons* (1956)
Sheila Birkenhead: *Peace in Piccadilly* (1958)

St. James's Park

Beatrice Curtis Brown: *Southwards from Swiss Cottage* (1947)
Elizabeth Myers: *Basilisk of St. James's* (1945)
Walter Besant: *Westminster* (1907)
Francis Bond: *Westminster Abbey* (1909)
W. G. Bell: *Tower of London* (1921)
Arthur Mee: *London* (1937)
Aytoun Ellis: *Penny Universities* (1956)
John Summerson: *John Nash* (1949)
J. W. Robertson Scott: *The Story of the Pall Mall Gazette* (1950)
J. W. Robertson Scott: *The Life and Death of a Newspaper* (1952)
Patrick Braybrooke: *A Life of John Morley* (1924)
David Jones: *The Anathemata* (1952)
Alfred Werner: *Moths and Butterflies* (1956)
Brian Hill: *Pleasure Garden* (1956)
Everyman Anthology of British Orations (1937)
Eric de Maré: *London's Riverside* (1958)

INDEX

A page number followed by (s) denotes a statue. Where confusion may arise, as in the case of the 'Cake House' and 'Cheesecake House', an initial indicates in which park it is to be found.

. . . Imperfections may occasion perfection; which makes me to hope that hereafter the defects of this my book (without prejudice to my profit or credit) will be judiciously discovered, and industriously ammended by others.

From *The Worthies of England*, by THOMAS FULLER (1662).